Fault Diagnosis of Digital Systems

FAULT DIAGNOSIS

OF

DIGITAL SYSTEMS

Herbert Y. Chang

Bell Telephone Laboratories, Inc.

Eric Manning

University of Waterloo
formerly, Bell Telephone Laboratories, Inc.

Gernot Metze

University of Illinois

WILEY-INTERSCIENCE

A DIVISION OF JOHN WILEY & SONS

NEW YORK · LONDON · SYDNEY · TORONTO

To the memory of
PROFESSOR SUNDARAM SESHU,
teacher, counselor, and friend

Foreword

This book deals with a new topic in Computer Science—automatic diagnosis of faults in digital systems. The plan for this book was first conceived at the time of Sundaram Seshu's death in an automobile accident in 1965, by some of his friends who were searching for ways to perpetuate his memory. His work had concentrated on the problem of automatic diagnosis of faults in digital systems. The intensity of his work in this area had influenced colleagues and students alike; a "school of thought" was in the process of formation. His untimely death interrupted this process, and many of the results of his studies were left unpublished. Clearly, there was an opportunity and an obligation to make these results known.

It is fitting that this book has been written by three of the people most closely associated with Seshu at the time of his death. Drs. Chang and Manning were his students, and Dr. Metze was a close collaborator in many of his studies. Their original objective was to simply write a research monograph on specific topics, aiming to preserve Seshu's ideas and approaches to the fault diagnosis problem. However, as the writing proceeded, this objective was substantially enlarged. As a result, the monograph is essentially self contained, incorporating the work of the authors and of many other workers, as well as Seshu's contributions. After mastering this book a reader should be able to understand the current literature and apply it to the solution of problems.

As one privileged to have associated with Seshu for more than a decade, I am pleased to record a few facts about the man to whose memory this book is dedicated. Seshu was a native of Madras, India, and he received his education in India to the M.S. level. He came to the United States in 1952, enrolling in the Ph.D. program at the University of Illinois where he received his degree in 1955. Although he left the University of Illinois for appointments at Syracuse University and the University of Toronto, he never lost touch with his students and colleagues at Illinois. He returned on a permanent basis in 1961. He was a man of enormous energy and dedication. This self-discipline was fabulous, and he devoted most of his waking hours to his work. To his students and associates, he was a warm, human, emotional individual, never too busy to listen to a problem or to help find solutions. This intense loyalty to friends extended to his profession and to the University.

As Seshu was a pioneer in fault diagnosis, so this book is the first to be published on this new topic in Computer Science, a topic that will grow in importance with Computer Science.

M. E. Van Valkenburg
Princeton University

Preface

This book deals with the diagnosis of hardware faults in digital systems. We would like to describe how and why it came to exist in its present form.

The reliability and availability of computing systems have become topics of prime concern. Of the two major techniques available to increase availability, the use of redundancy has received far more publicity than the other approach—the use of automatic fault diagnosis. Although considerable work has been done in fault diagnosis, the results are scattered among various technical journals, conference digests, and internal reports. Therefore, we saw a need for at least one book that would gather these results and present them in a unified way.

This immediately raised a problem: should the book be an authoritative treatise or a less ambitious research monograph? Fault diagnosis is a very new topic in the infant discipline of computer science. It is barely ten years old, and its concepts and methods are still changing rapidly. Moreover, many of its central problems are still unsolved. Thus, we felt that a treatise would be premature, and we elected to write a research monograph.

This monograph is a summary of the research results that seemed most important to us; we have also tried to give the reader a "set of pointers" to the literature. (Consequently, we have chosen more or less to stay with the notations of cited references, to make it easier for the reader to study them.) We have not written a "cookbook" for maintenance technicians, nor have we written a critical survey for the specialist in fault diagnosis. Instead, we have written for graduate students and workers who are active in other areas of computer science. We have tried to provide, for these groups, an introduction to fault diagnosis that will be as quick and painless as possible. We hope they will be able to read and understand the literature after studying this book.

We began to write in the fall of 1967, with every intention of including a representative set of timely and important contributions. Needless to say, several good papers appeared after the manuscript was finished. These are not discussed in the text, but we have included them in the references. Our division of responsibility in writing the book is as follows.

Chapter II (Background) Chapter V (Fault Dictionaries), and Section 3.3 (Methods of Test Minimization) are the work of Chang.

Chapter IV (The Sequential Analyzer), Section 3.1 (Methods of Test Generation—Combinational Circuits), Section 6.2 (Recent Developments), and Section 6.3 (Speculations) were written by Manning.

Section 3.4 (Methods of Fault Simulation) and Section 6.1 (Recent Developments in Digital Fault Simulation) were written by Chang and Manning.

Finally, Section 3.2 (Methods of Test Generation—Sequential Circuits) and Chapter I were jointly produced. All of us, of course, are responsible for technical and stylistic blunders.

The first draft of the manuscript evolved from a set of class notes used by Chang and Manning in a graduate course given at Bell Telephone Laboratories in Naperville, Illinois. It proved suitable for a one-semester course at the senior or graduate level in computer science.

We are indebted to many people at Bell Laboratories for their help in making this book possible. Particularly, we are grateful to Frank Goetz and Werner Ulrich for their continual support. We are also greatly indebted to Mrs. Lily Seshu, whose encouragement led us to undertake the project. Finally, the excellent typing done by Mrs. Shelvia Mounce and Miss Mary Warner is gratefully acknowledged.

Herbert Y. Chang
Eric G. Manning
Gernot Metze

November 1968

Contents

Fault Diagnosis of Digital Systems

CHAPTER I

Introduction

As the range of problems to which digital computing systems have been applied has widened, the task of ensuring that a computer system is operating correctly has become steadily more important. In the past, computers were used largely in an off-line, batch-processing mode, and the consequences of undetected hardware malfunctions were relatively minor. We now see increasing use of computers in on-line, real-time applications such as the control of chemical process units and nuclear reactors, and military command and control. Incorrect computer operation in any of these applications can be potentially disastrous. At the same time, the increasing size and complexity of digital computers have made it more and more difficult to ensure correct machine operation.

There are two fundamentally different ways of coping with component faults, and either way can be implemented with hardware, software, or both. The effects of the fault can be masked by some sort of redundancy technique, or the presence of the fault can be detected by a diagnosis procedure. Fault-masking serves to postpone the inevitable; given sufficient time, enough failures will occur to overwhelm the masking facility. Hence it is useful primarily in such applications as spacecraft guidance, where correct operation of the system must be guaranteed for a relatively short period of time and repair is difficult or impossible. Fault diagnosis plus repair, on the other hand, is useful when machine outages can be tolerated but faults should not go undetected. This is the case in an off-line batch-processing installation. Although it is inconvenient to the user and embarrassing to the supplier of batch processing service, jobs can be reprocessed after detection and repair of a fault with no great penalty.

In one sense, fault-masking and fault diagnosis are incompatible, since the effects of a masked fault cannot be observed or diagnosed—at least until a further fault develops in the masking mechanism. However, many ingenious ways of using redundancy so that redundant mechanisms can be made non-redundant for test purposes have been developed. This allows us to combine

1

fault-masking and fault diagnosis technologies. The combination is exactly what is needed for such applications as real-time control of processes and on-line information processing (information retrieval systems and the coming computer utilities); it is essential in these applications to prevent any total system outage over a very long system lifetime. This means that redundancy must be employed to permit the system to operate correctly in the presence of a fault. It also means that fault detection and diagnosis must be employed, so that faults can be rapidly repaired. Otherwise the fault-masking apparatus will eventually become swamped with faults.

Although fault-masking and fault-diagnosis techniques are both essential ingredients of an on-line, real-time system, it appears that redundancy technology has received far more attention than has diagnosis. Hence this book.

A glance at the history of fault diagnosis reveals that the earliest computers were maintained by highly skilled technicians, who used intuitive procedures based on their "clinical experience" with the system in question. So-called diagnostic programs were used as an aid, but the inadequacies of these placed the major burden squarely on the technician's shoulders. It is hard to accumulate "clinical experience" with modern digital systems, partly because such experience is not easy to communicate from man to man, partly because new circuitries are continually being introduced, and, para-doxically, because modern components rarely fail.

Fault diagnosis in modern systems is further complicated by the growing popularity of integrated circuitry, which makes the probing of circuits for signals at internal points impossible. Even the provision of many test points is impractical. Hence, test procedures are required which use only the normal inputs and outputs of a circuit to derive information about the presence and location of faults. Notice that a circuit may well be several hundreds of logic gates.

We also require that procedures be highly automated. Rapid reconfigura-tion of a system to establish a working subsystem with no interruption of service requires that fault detection be done at electronic speeds.

The main topic of this book, therefore, is the development of techniques for the generation, selection, and evaluation of automated diagnosis pro-cedures for digital systems. These techniques must cope with both sequential and combinational circuits, and must use only the normally accessible ter-minals of the circuits comprising the system. The primary tool used in these techniques is computer simulation of the failure-free circuit and of the circuits created from it by the occurrence of failures.

Chapter II presents basic definitions and assumptions needed to establish mathematical models of a logic circuit under failure, and reviews early approaches to the diagnosis problem. Certain results from other disciplines are outlined which are prerequisite to the material of later chapters. In Chapter III, methods of deriving and selecting tests for combinational and sequential circuits are given. A brief account of techniques developed by International Business Machines to handle a special class of very large sequential circuits (the processors of the IBM System/360 line) is also presented.

Chapter IV contains a discussion of the Sequential Analyzer, a system of computer programs for generating and simulating tests for logic circuits. The Analyzer is representative of modern digital fault simulators in its ability to simulate combinational and sequential circuits with failures, but is unique in its ability to automatically generate test sequences for a logic circuit. A discussion of Analyzer applications is given, followed by a critique of the present programs based on the experience gained from these applications. Since much of the material presented in the previous chapters is essential for a good understanding of the Analyzer, Chapter IV unifies the topics discussed in the first part of the book.

Once a set of diagnostics has been developed with the aid of some sort of simulator, it is necessary to find ways of interpreting the results generated by use of the diagnostics, to yield repair information. Ways of doing this are discussed in Chapter V. In the final chapter, we outline some current research problems. These include: improved simulation techniques aimed at overcoming the shortcomings of present-day fault simulators; the development of design principles to yield more diagnosable digital systems; the development of languages for describing digital systems on functional and higher levels; and the automatic compilation of system designs. We close with a section on unsolved problems.

CHAPTER II

Background

In this chapter we briefly summarize the background material necessary for a complete understanding of the book. Our treatment is much too brief to allow the reader to remedy any deficiencies by studying this material alone. Therefore, the material should be supplemented by consulting the cited references.

The background material falls into three categories: (1) definitions and models, (2) historical material, and (3) results from automata theory and the theory of testing. Section 2.1 contains elementary definitions and models. Basic definitions concerning digital systems, combinational and sequential circuits, and failure modes of electronic digital circuitry are given. We also outline the Moore and Mealy models for synchronous sequential circuits, the Huffman model for asynchronous sequential circuits, and introduce the notion of *test*. This material is especially important for an understanding of the rest of the book.

The historical material of Section 2.2 is not essential, but should help the reader to place this book in correct perspective. Our aim is to show how fault diagnosis emerged as an important problem, and how the early attempts at solutions grew. Finally, Section 2.3 outlines Moore's notion of gedanken-experiments, and some fundamental ideas about methods of testing equipment in general. This material is as essential as the contents of Section 2.1 to a good grasp of the rest of the book.

2.1 Definitions and Assumptions

2.1.1 Digital Systems. The phrase *digital system* is generally used to denote an interconnected set of elements that process discrete, finite-valued signals. Electronic digital computers, telephone switching systems, and digital control systems are all examples of digital systems. Techniques for the analysis and synthesis of digital systems have been developed within the

4

theory of switching circuits. Hence, people often think of a digital system as an interconnection of combinational switching circuits and sequential switching circuits.[1]

A switching circuit is *combinational* if its outputs $z_1, \ldots, z_m$ can be written as Boolean functions of its inputs $x_1, \ldots, x_n$:

$$z_1 = a_1(x_1, \ldots, x_n),$$
$$z_2 = a_2(x_1, \ldots, x_n),$$
$$\cdots\cdots\cdots\cdots\cdots\cdots$$
$$z_m = a_m(x_1, \ldots, x_n); \tag{2.1}$$

or, more compactly,

$$\mathbf{Z} = \mathbf{A(X)}.$$

A block diagram for combinational circuits is shown in Figure 2.1.

A switching circuit is *sequential* if its output values at a given time depend not only on the present inputs but also on inputs applied previously. The history of previous inputs is summarized in the *state* $\mathbf{S}$ of the circuit.[2] Thus we have

$$\mathbf{Z} = \mathbf{A(X; S)} \tag{2.2}$$

for a sequential circuit, where $\mathbf{A}$ is a vector-valued function of vector arguments as before. A block diagram for sequential circuits is shown in Figure 2.2. The circuit of Figure 2.2 has n primary inputs $x_1, \ldots, x_n$; m primary outputs $z_1, \ldots, z_m$; and p feedback outputs $Y_1, \ldots, Y_p$. There are two basically different kinds of sequential circuits; *synchronous sequential circuits* and *asynchronous sequential circuits*. For a synchronous circuit, the primary outputs $\mathbf{Z}$ and feedback outputs $\mathbf{Y}$ can be written as Boolean functions of the primary inputs $\mathbf{X}$ and feedback inputs $\mathbf{y}$:

$$\mathbf{Z}_t = \mathbf{A}_t(\mathbf{X; y})$$
$$\mathbf{Y}_t = \mathbf{B}_t(\mathbf{X; y}). \tag{2.3}$$
$$\mathbf{y}_{t+1} = \mathbf{Y}_t$$

This is the model of synchronous circuit behavior due to Mealy (1955). The other common model for synchronous circuits is Moore's (1956), where

$$\mathbf{Z}_t = \mathbf{A}_t(\mathbf{y})$$
$$\mathbf{Y}_t = \mathbf{B}_t(\mathbf{X; y}) \tag{2.4}$$
$$\mathbf{y}_{t+1} = \mathbf{Y}_t$$

---

[1] We often use the words *circuit* and *system* in this book to refer to "small" and "large" networks, respectively. The meaning of "small" and "large" in any such usage should be clear from the context.

[2] General treatments of the notion of *state* can be found in many standard texts on switching theory (see the references at the end of the book).

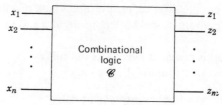

Figure 2.1   Block diagram of a combinational circuit.

As usual, $\mathbf{A}$ and $\mathbf{B}$ are vector-valued functions of vector arguments. In both cases, the subscripts t and $t + 1$ imply that the circuit's behavior is clocked at discrete instants of time. Indeed, the above quantities are defined only at the discrete instants of time $t = 0, 1, 2, \ldots$. Stated another way, the primary outputs and feedback outputs at the present time t are determined by the primary and feedback inputs at t. The present feedback output vector $\mathbf{Y}_t$ will, in turn, after some delay in the memory elements, become the feedback input vector $\mathbf{y}_{t+1}$ for the next time instant, $t + 1$.

A comparison of equations 2.2 and 2.3 suggests that the feedback input vector $\mathbf{y}$ represents the state $\mathbf{S}$ of the circuit. This, in fact, is true; indeed, $\mathbf{y}$ and $\mathbf{Y}$ are often called the *present state* and *next state* of the circuit. Notice also that our models assume that all internal delay resides in the feedback lines and that the combinational part of the model reacts instantaneously to its inputs $\mathbf{X}$ and $\mathbf{y}$. This model is a valid representation of noninstantaneous circuitry, provided that the feedback delay is greater than the worst-case combination of delays in the combinational part. A block diagram for either synchronous model is shown in Figure 2.3.

The behavior of an asynchronous circuit is not synchronized, and there is therefore no external clock. Each feedback line is assumed to have a finite, positive, pure delay, as is shown in Figure 2.4. The following conditions are required to ensure proper operation of an asynchronous circuit.

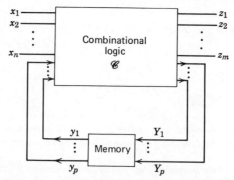

Figure 2.2   Block diagram of a sequential circuit.

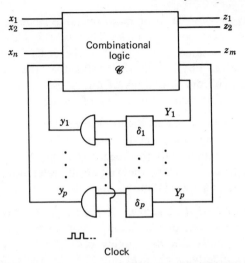

Figure 2.3   Block diagram of a synchronous sequential circuit.

1. The combinational logic is assumed to be hazard-free and the circuit is permitted to settle down before the next input change occurs.

2. Successive inputs must be *adjacent* (must differ in exactly one bit from each other).

3. There can be no oscillations. Thus, application of any legitimate input to the circuit in any present *stable state*[3] must cause it eventually to enter some stable state. This condition therefore guarantees *existence* of the next stable state.

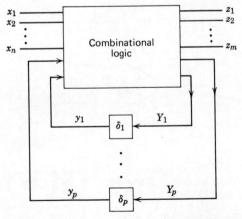

Figure 2.4   Block diagram of an asynchronous sequential circuit.

[3] Stable states are those for which $y = Y$.

4. There may be *races* (two or more unstable feedback lines[4] at a given time), but these must not be *critical*. That is, the stable state eventually reached must be the same, independent of the order in which the unstable lines become stable. Physically, this means that the next stable state is invariant under arbitrary variations of any subset of the delays $\{\delta_j\}$. This condition therefore guarantees *uniqueness* of the next stable state.

We shall refer to the above model as Huffman's model, since it appears to have been implicitly introduced by Huffman (1954). Once again, if all of this is not thoroughly familiar to the reader, he should consult any current textbook on sequential machine theory (see the references, p. 151) or Huffman's classic paper. Chapter IV of this book draws heavily on these concepts.

2.1.2   Faults of Digital Circuitry.   A *fault* or *failure*[5] of a digital circuit is a physical defect of one or more components, which can cause the circuit to malfunction. Faults can be roughly classified into several categories, according to the underlying physical causes. Aging or manufacturing defects can cause a component to gradually deteriorate, giving rise to *marginal* faults. Critical timing, noise, and overly close tolerances can cause *intermittent* faults. Here the fault is time-varying, being present in some intervals of time and absent in others. Many faults that originally are intermittent eventually become *solid*. This implies that the malfunction is permanent until repairs are made. For example, a permanently open collector or base lead of a transistor is a solid fault, as shown in Figure 2.5. Under these faults, the transistor output Q would appear to be permanently stuck-at-high. On the other hand,

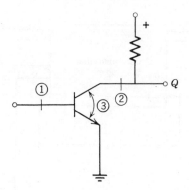

Figure 2.5 Some failure modes of a transistor. ① Base open. ② Collector open. ③ Collector-to-emitter short.

[4] The *j*th feedback line is unstable iff $y_j \neq Y_j$.
[5] Muller (1967) has discussed the interrelationships between the notions of *fault, failure,* and *malfunction* with great care. Notice that we use *fault* and *failure* as synonyms in this book, rather than preserve one of Muller's distinctions.

a short from the collector to the emitter would cause Q to appear to be permanently stuck-at-low. Many failures of digital circuits create stuck-at-high or stuck-at-low conditions. These faults are collectively called *logical faults*. Most of our techniques for analyzing system behavior under failure assume logical faults. Therefore, all discussion in this book is confined to solid, logical faults unless otherwise stated. Our restriction is based on the limitations of our techniques rather than on their adequacy. Thus methods for treating marginal, intermittent, or nonlogical faults are necessary topics for future research.

Although methods for analyzing system behavior under failure form a large part of this book, a brief example to convey the "flavor" might be helpful here. Consider the AND gate shown in Figure 2.6. In the absence of failures, the output signal Q realizes the Boolean function

$$Q = x_1 \cdot x_2 \cdot x_3$$

of the input signal variables. If the diode at input x_1 is opened, the AND gate will obviously function as though the x_1 input were not present. In other words, the variable x_1 will appear to be permanently stuck-at-one (s–a–1). Hence

$$Q\big|_{x_1=1} = 1 \cdot x_2 \cdot x_3 = x_2 \cdot x_3$$

Indeed, this fault is often referred to simply as the "x_1 s–a–1 fault." In the same vein, the collector-emitter short of the transistor is often called a "Q s–a–0 fault."

2.1.3 Tests. Here, we introduce some rudimentary notions and definitions concerning tests. Our purpose is to prepare the reader for Subsection

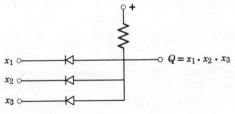

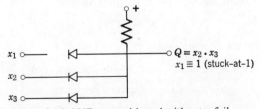

Figure 2.6 AND gate with and without a failure.

2.3.2, where some more interesting results from the theory of testing are presented.

To ensure proper operation of a system, we must be able to detect faults when they have occurred. Also, we must be able to pinpoint the locations of faults accurately enough to permit repair. We accomplish both tasks with tests. A *test* T_k is a sequence of input vectors $\mathbf{X}_{k1}, \ldots, \mathbf{X}_{ks}$ to be applied to the circuit, together with the corresponding circuit output vectors. The *length* of the test is the integer s. If several tests are required, they are collectively referred to as a *test set* or a *test sequence*. (The latter term is used if the tests must be applied in a specific order.) The circuit or system undergoing test is called the *subject*.

There are two kinds of tests: fault *detection* tests and fault *diagnostic* tests. A fault detection test has only two possible outcomes:

1. The subject has none of the faults of the prescribed class; or
2. The subject has some (unspecified) one of the prescribed class of faults.

Thus, consider the test of length 1:

$$T_k = \{\mathbf{X}_{k1}; \mathbf{Z}_{k1}\}.$$

This notation means that application of $\mathbf{X}_{k1}$ to the subject without failures yields the outputs $\mathbf{Z}_{k1}$. Now suppose that some fault f causes the outputs $\mathbf{Z}_{k1}$ to become $\mathbf{W}_{k1}$, where

$$\mathbf{W}_{k1} \neq \mathbf{Z}_{k1}.$$

Then test T_k is said to *detect* fault f, for we can determine whether f is present or absent by the use of T_k. If the subject is a sequential circuit, it is often necessary to use tests of length greater than one. Here, then, if

$$T_k = \{\mathbf{X}_{k1}, \ldots, \mathbf{X}_{ks}; \mathbf{Z}_{k1}, \ldots, \mathbf{Z}_{ks}\},$$

T_k will detect f if the sequence of output vectors with f differs at any point from $\mathbf{Z}_{k1}, \ldots, \mathbf{Z}_{ks}$.

Truth tables provide one common method of deriving tests for small combinational circuits. For example, consider an AND gate with inputs x_1 and x_2, and output z_1. The truth tables for the failure-free gate and for the gate with failure "x_1 s–a–1" are shown in Table 2.1(a) and (b). By comparing these tables, you can see that the test input vector

$$\mathbf{X} = (0, 1)$$

detects the fault, the output being

$$z_1 = 0 \qquad \text{(failure absent), and}$$
$$z_1 = 1 \qquad \text{(failure present).}$$

As another small example, consider the truth table for the same gate and the

Table 2.1 Truth Tables for a Two-Input AND Gate—(*a*) Normal; (*b*) x_1 Stuck-at-1; and (*c*) z Stuck-at-1

x_1	x_2	z		x_1 (s–a–1)	x_2	z		x_1	x_2	z (s–a–1)
0	0	0		⏍1	0	0		0	0	⏍1
0	1	0		⏍1	1	⏍1		0	1	⏍1
1	0	0		1	0	0		1	0	⏍1
1	1	1		1	1	1		1	1	1

fault "z_1 s–a–1." This is given in Table 2.1(*c*) and shows that the fault can be detected by any of the vectors

$$\mathbf{X} = (0, 1), \qquad \mathbf{X} = (1, 0), \qquad \text{and} \qquad \mathbf{X} = (0, 0).$$

Together, these two examples also show that a given fault may be detected by many tests, and that a given test may detect many faults. A set of tests that detects *every* fault of a prescribed class for some subject is called a *complete* test set for that subject.

In summary, fault detection tests only tell us whether a system is faulty or failure-free. They tell us nothing about the identity of a fault if one is present. A test that provides such information is called a *diagnostic* test. The quantity of information provided, crudely speaking, is called the *diagnostic resolution* of the test. Thus, a fault detection test is a fault diagnostic test of zero diagnostic resolution.

If the subject is built with discrete-component technology, we may need to identify faults down to the level of individual transistors or diodes. Hence we would demand a set of diagnostic tests having very high diagnostic resolution indeed. At the other extreme, Large-Scale Integration (LSI) technology may some day give us entire subjects on single, replaceable circuit packages. In this event, zero diagnostic resolution (fault detection tests only) would suffice. Repair would be achieved by simply replacing the entire subject and discarding the failed one!

Perhaps a short example will crystallize these ideas. Referring once again to Table 2.1, the test

$$\mathbf{X} = (0, 1)$$

detects both the x_1 s–a–1 fault and the z_1 s–a–1 fault. However, it does not distinguish between them, since the circuit output is 1 for both faults. Thus, if we wished to isolate faults only to the level of gates, this would be an adequate diagnostic test for both faults. On the other hand, if we wished to isolate faults down to the level of individual transistors and diodes, we would

Table 2.2   Test Outcomes

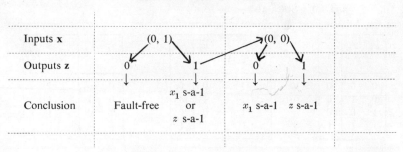

Inputs x	(0, 1)		(0, 0)	
Outputs z	0	1	0	1
	↓	↓	↓	↓
Conclusion	Fault-free	x_1 s-a-1 or z s-a-1	x_1 s-a-1	z s-a-1

have to add another test input vector to the test. In fact, the test of length 2,

$$T = \{(0, 1), (0, 0); (0), (0)\},$$

suffices. The test outputs for the faults are illustrated in Table 2.2. Generally, the length of a test grows with the diagnostic resolution that it must provide.

2.2   Historical Background

In this section, we try to trace the emergence of fault diagnosis as an important problem, and sketch the early attempts at solutions. Our account begins with the appearance of the first electronic digital computers, around 1950.

Many of the earliest machines used a combination of skilled maintenance technicians and special hardware to diagnose faults. Built-in voltmeters, test oscilloscopes, and checking circuits were fairly common. This approach was perhaps developed most fully in the BINAC computer, described by Eckert (1953). BINAC had two complete, identical processors that performed all computations in synchronism. The actions of the processors were continually compared by match circuits. The occurrence of a malfunction was detected by a mismatch, which caused both processors to be stopped immediately. The propagation of incorrect results was therefore held to a minimum, and the maintenance technician was able to examine the final states of the two processors to help him diagnose the fault.

In addition to special hardware, many early machines made limited use of test programs. These usually were used to help the technician to cope with intermittent or marginal faults. The cyclic program control used in WHIRL-WIND (Daggett and Rich, 1953) provides one example. This technique allowed the technician to repeatedly execute a selected sequence of machine code via a stop-restart control. He could monitor certain test points while this was done, so as to track down elusive marginal or intermittent faults.

EDSAC used an automatic routing procedure, which permitted the execution of test programs with or without voltage margins. This technique, described by Wilkes et al. (1953), was often of considerable help in locating marginal failures. Nevertheless, all of these machines relied heavily on the skill and detailed knowledge of the maintenance technician. He had to be thoroughly familiar with the logical and circuit design of the machine, and also had to make adjustments, initiate testing, and interpret the test results manually. As systems grew in size and complexity, this approach obviously became less and less practical.

Consequently, as machines became larger and more complex, special-purpose test instruments and hardware moved from center stage to a supporting rôle. The main burden came to be placed more and more on *diagnostic programs*, which rapidly became the prime troubleshooting tool. The earliest programs were written to exercise machine *functions*, rather than *hardware*. The general approach was first to execute a complex machine instruction (such as MULTIPLY) by using pseudorandom operands. The results were then compared with those obtained by using an equivalent sequence of simpler instructions (say, ADD and SHIFT) but the same operands. If the results agreed, the complex instruction was assumed to be operative and, if otherwise, it was assumed to be defective. Now one (or even several) sets of pseudorandom operands cannot possibly provide a complete functional test of a complex device such as an arithmetic unit. Furthermore, the instruction under test is almost never hardware-disjoint from the instructions of the equivalent sequence. Finally, a disagreement may well be caused by malfunction of some instruction of the equivalent sequence. Thus the conclusion is not necessarily valid. This is borne out by experiences reported by Walters (1953), Estrin (1953), and Meagher and Nash (1952).

The key to a major improvement lay in testing machine *hardware* rather than functions.[6] The first study to exploit this approach was by Eldred (1959). His results, which are described in Section 3.1, were used to derive the diagnostic program for the Datamatic-1000 processor. Subsequently, hardware-oriented diagnostics came into general use and are still used today.

The need for effective diagnosis procedures increased sharply in the early 1960s, with the advent of real-time and time-shared computer applications.

---

[6] Nothing is wrong with the concept *per se* of testing system functions; the issues here are completeness and diagnostic resolution. For example, a complete functional test of a 32-bit adder requires 2^{64} operations, and provides very little information about the location of the fault. A hardware-oriented test of a binary ripple-carry adder, using full adder stages, can be done in 8 operations with good diagnostic resolution (Marlett, 1966). In modern practice, therefore, functional testing is usually restricted to units such as registers and flip-flops, whose functions are simple enough to permit complete functional testing. The remainder of the subject is treated by hardware-oriented testing. An early example of this mixture of approaches was given by Bashkow et al. (1963).

For these applications, one must be able to detect faults with a very high degree of certainty, and must be able to repair the system rapidly. Indeed, in the case of real-time, time-shared operation of computers to perform tasks such as telephone switching, one must also reconfigure the system at electronic speed so that *no* interruption of service results. Examples of such systems are discussed by Downing et al. (1964) and by Suda (1967).

These new constraints gave much of the impetus to the development of our current fault diagnosis technology. It is this technology that we discuss in the remainder of the book.

2.3   Analytical Background

Here we discuss some general ideas related to fault diagnosis. Our material is taken largely from the works of Moore (1956) and Johnson et al. (1959). In this discussion, we have in mind the general experimental setup of Figure 2.7. Here, the test routines are first derived, formally or intuitively, from

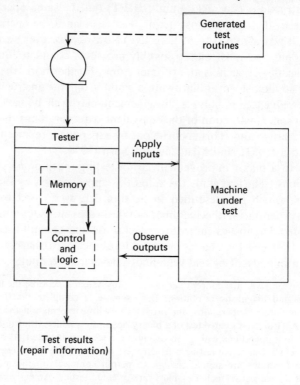

Figure 2.7   Application of tests.

information about the subject. Then they are loaded into the tester. The tester must be capable (1) of applying stimuli to the subject (the machine under test), (2) of observing the responses elicited by these stimuli, and (3) of making decisions, based on the observed responses, as to the next stimuli to be applied. The tester is often a computer or some sort of computerlike entity.

Observe that this model of the testing process is somewhat general. Thus the subject could be any of the following.

1. A television set, in which case the tester would be a TV repairman (the test routines would be derived very intuitively, indeed).

2. A large, newly built computer sitting on the factory floor, in which case the tester would probably be a small computer.

3. The central processor of an electronic switching system, in which case the tester would possibly be an identical copy of the subject, coupled to it by match circuits and shared memory.

4. The distinction between subject and tester could become blurred, with most of the tester's functions migrating into *the subject itself*, and the residue going to a human operator. This possibility (computer self-diagnosis) is discussed in Subsections 3.2.3 and 4.4.2.

2.3.1   Gedanken-Experiments.   Many fundamental ideas about testing can be expressed neatly in terms of the *gedanken-experiments* of Moore (1956). Here, a machine is considered to be a black box with input and output terminals. We attempt to learn as much as possible about the contents of the box by performing mental[7] experiments on the input and output terminals only—prying off the lid of the box is forbidden. Thus the gedanken-experimenter is a person or another machine that tries to study the behavior of the black box by applying sequences of input stimuli and observing output responses.

There are two kinds of gedanken-experiments: *simple* experiments and *multiple* experiments. The simple experiment is shown in Figure 2.8. Here, the machine receives a sequence of inputs (stimuli) from the experimenter and produces a sequence of responses. (If the machine is deterministic, each response is determined by the corresponding stimulus and the current state of the machine.) Having observed the responses, the experimenter either will choose another sequence of stimuli to apply to the machine or will draw some conclusion about the machine, or both. In addition to a great many other situations (e.g., certain experimental situations in the physical and behavioral sciences) the simple experiment provides an abstract model for the testing process of Figure 2.7.

---

[7] Cf. the German *gedanken*, or thought.

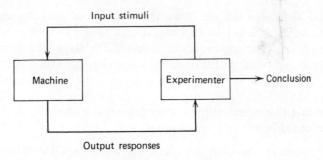

Figure 2.8 Simple gedanken-experiment.

The second kind of gedanken-experiment—the multiple experiment—is shown in Figure 2.9. Here, the experimenter is provided with several copies of the machine, all of which are in the same state at the beginning of the experiment. The experimenter sends sequences of input stimuli to the copies of the machine, and receives the corresponding response sequence from each copy. Notice that the input sequences (and, hence, the output sequences) may be different for the different copies of the machine. Based on the responses, the experimenter may choose to apply additional sequences of stimuli to the various copies, or he (or it) may draw inferences about their common internal structure. We now attempt to show how multiple gedanken-experiments, too, are relevant to fault diagnosis.

Suppose that we have a digital system, which can suffer any one of n permissible faults. Suppose further that insertion of any one of the permissible faults into the fault-free system creates a new digital system. Then we may think of the $n + 1$ systems thus created as being the machine copies of a multiple gedanken-experiment. Application of a stimulus, and observation of the responses of this set of $n + 1$ machines, induces a *partition* with respect

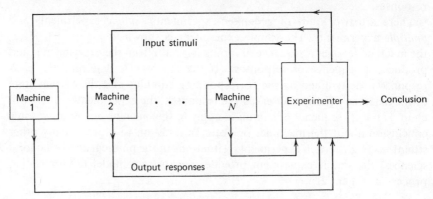

Figure 2.9 Multiple gedanken-experiment.

to observed responses on the set of machines. That is, all machines that exhibit the same response are grouped together to form an equivalence class. The collection of equivalence classes thus obtained defines a partition on the set of machines. Further experimentation will serve to *refine* the initial partition of machines. (This process can be graphically represented as a *test diagram* or *diagnostic tree*, as is discussed in Subsection 2.3.2). Viewed from the standpoint of multiple gedanken-experiments, therefore, a *fault detection test* is simply a multiple experiment that produces a final partition of machines, so that the fault-free machine is the only member of some partition block. Similarly, a *fault diagnosis test* of maximal diagnostic resolution corresponds to a final partition of machines having exactly one machine per block.

In summary, then, the concept of associating a failed machine with each permissible fault of the subject allows us to formulate a number of concepts in fault diagnosis in terms of Moore's multiple gedanken-experiments. This formulation provides the conceptual foundation for the Sequential Analyzer, to which Chapter IV of this book is devoted.

2.3.2 Testing Procedures. There are two major kinds of *testing procedures: sequential* procedures and *combinational* procedures. For a sequential procedure, the jth test input vector is determined from the responses elicited by the previous $j - 1$ input vectors. This is not the case for a combinational procedure; the jth input vector is specified regardless of the subject's previous responses. Observe that either kind of procedure (sequential or combinational) could be applied to either kind of subject circuit (sequential or combinational).

To obtain a test procedure of either kind, we must determine the response of the subject to a given test input vector, in the presence of a given fault. The process of doing this is called *fault simulation*, and is discussed in Section 3.4. The result of fault simulation is a mapping from fault identities to test outcomes, called the *simulation data*. The simulation data can be greatly simplified by merely recording the tests that detect each permissible fault. Thus

$$\{(f_i; T_{1i}, T_{2i}, \ldots, T_{ni})\} \qquad \forall \ f_i \text{ in the set of permissible faults,}$$

is a simplified representation of the simulation data; and says that tests

$$T_{1i}, T_{2i}, \ldots, T_{ni}$$

detect fault f_i. Bear in mind that a test T_k, as defined in Section 2.1, may be a *sequence* of test input and test output vectors. Furthermore, each test must begin by resetting the subject to a fixed, known, initial state.

(a) Sequential Testing Procedures. Sequential testing procedures are much more common in practice than are combinational procedures. A sequential

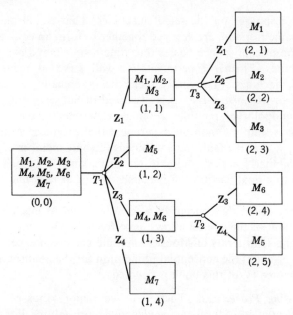

Figure 2.10   Test diagram for a sequential procedure.

testing procedure can be graphically represented as a diagnostic tree, as is shown in Figure 2.10. This test diagram is derived from the simulation data of Table 2.3. Each fault corresponds to one branch of the tree (but not necessarily conversely) and the *leaves* (branch terminations) correspond to places where testing is halted. The failure-free machine is always M_1, by convention, and is always carried in the uppermost branch of the tree. Furthermore, the vertices of the tree are coordinatized in an obvious way.

The diagram of Figure 2.10 says, then, that test T_1, when applied to the good machine and the six machines with failures, creates a partition of machines having four blocks. These blocks, or *equivalence classes*, are (M_1, M_2, M_3), (M_5), (M_4, M_6) and (M_7). Tests T_2 and T_3 are then used to further partition the blocks (M_1, M_2, M_3) and (M_4, M_6). Notice, in this case, that every branch of the tree (or sequence of test inputs and outputs) serves

Table 2.3   Simulation Data for Three Tests

	z_1	z_2	z_3	z_4
T_1	M_1, M_2, M_3	M_5	M_4, M_6	M_7
T_2	M_1, M_2, M_3	M_5, M_7	M_6	M_4
T_3	M_1	M_2, M_4, M_5 M_6, M_7	M_3	—

to uniquely identify one machine. Thus we have a sequential test procedure of maximal diagnostic resolution.

A test diagram can be constructed simply by invoking the knowledge of an experienced maintenance technician. However, the diagram would, of course, represent the steps that the technician would have followed to diagnose the circuit manually. Such procedures are often very inefficient.[8]

The more formal methods for constructing a test diagram generally use some sort of figure of merit, which assigns numerical estimates to the relative "significance" of tests. At each vertex of the tree, several candidate tests are evaluated and the one of greatest "significance" is chosen. The process is repeated until adequate fault detection and diagnostic resolution have been obtained. This process provides local optimization only, but global optimization is usually impractical for all but the simplest subjects. We shall pursue these ideas further in Section 3.3.

(*b*) *Combinational Testing Procedures.* The choice of combinational testing procedures over sequential ones tends to reduce the amount of data stored in the tester. They are therefore helpful in applications where storage is at a premium. Hence they have been relatively unpopular with the current generation of general-purpose computers, but they are used widely in electronic telephone-switching machines. The fact that all tests are always run means that the average time to diagnose a fault is higher than for a sequential procedure. It also means that the diagnosis procedure has redundancy—more tests are usually applied than are strictly required.

If all of our assumptions about permissible failure modes were always valid, this fact would offer no advantage. However, in reality, there is an advantage, since faults often do occur in the field which were not considered when the tests were generated. The redundancy inherent in combinational testing can often be used to allow us to diagnose these "forbidden" faults. Ways of doing this are described in Chapter V. In summary, then, the choice of combinational testing over sequential testing amounts to a trade-off of storage for time, with the added attraction of a capability for dealing with "forbidden" faults.

As we have stated, the tests are applied in a fixed order, thereby producing a pattern of test results. This pattern is then analyzed (usually by the maintenance man) by matching it against the patterns derived from fault simulation. A match points directly to the circuit package(s) to be replaced. To

---

[8] In another context, Seshu and Waxman (1966) have shown that technicians customarily use very inefficient methods to diagnose linear active circuits. For example, an audio amplifier is usually tested at audible frequencies, with an audio generator and voltmeter. Far more information per test can be obtained by using test signals near the breakpoints of the amplifier's response plot. These signals usually are at subaudible and superaudible frequencies.

Table 2.4   A Simple Type of Fault Dictionary

Tests T_1	T_2	T_3	T_4	T_5	Machines (Faults)
		.			.
		.			.
		.			.
0	0	1	0	0	M_i
0	1	0	0	0	M_{i+1}
1	0	0	1	1	M_{i+2}
		.			.
		.			.
		.			.

facilitate the process of pattern matching, the simulation data are processed to form the various fault dictionaries (see Chapter V). Among other attributes, the dictionaries are arranged to make matching easy.

The following example illustrates the use of combinational testing with a very simple type of fault dictionary. Suppose that the subject's responses to all tests, in the presence of each permissible fault, have been obtained by some fault simulation method. The simulation data could be processed to form the fault dictionary of Table 2.4. Here, the circuit output vectors have been replaced by simple pass-or-fail data. Thus, a "0" means that a test is passed (all circuit output vectors identical to those of the good machine), and a "1" means that a test is failed. Thus if a maintenance technician applies tests T_1, T_2, T_3, T_4, and T_5 in the field, and obtains the pattern of results

$$00100,$$

the failed machine is identified as M_i.

Notice that a combinational testing procedure can also be represented by a test diagram. In this case, all test input vectors at a given level of the diagram will be identical. For example, if the tests of Table 2.3 are applied in the fixed order

$$T_1 \to T_2 \to T_3,$$

the resulting combinational test procedure is given in Figure 2.11. A corresponding fault dictionary is given in Table 2.5. For this procedure, it is interesting to note that we do not need to apply all tests in order to diagnose certain faults (M_5 and M_7, for example). In fact, if either $\mathbf{Z}_2$ or $\mathbf{Z}_4$ is observed as output vector of test T_1, testing can be halted at once. (This is because the failed machine has already been identified as M_5 or M_7, respectively.) This trick is called *early termination*. A combinational procedure that has been

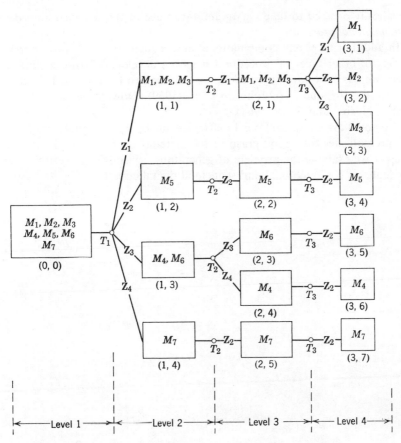

Figure 2.11 Test diagram for a combinational procedure.

Table 2.5 Fault Dictionary Corresponding to Figure 2.11

Tests			
T_1	T_2	T_3	Machines
z_1	z_1	z_1	M_1 $\leftarrow$ (Failure-free)
z_1	z_1	z_2	M_2 $\leftarrow$ (Failure)
z_1	z_1	z_3	M_3 .
z_2	z_2	z_2	M_5 .
z_3	z_3	z_2	M_6 .
z_3	z_4	z_2	M_4
z_4	z_2	z_2	M_7 $\leftarrow$ (Failure)

specifically ordered to take maximum advantage of this is called an *ordered combinational procedure.*

In addition to purely combinational and sequential testing procedures, a variety of other types of procedures has been developed. However, most of them are basically variants or mixtures of these two basic types. For further details, see the studies of Johnson et al. (1959), Downing et al. (1964), or Galey, Norby, and Roth (1964).

We now have completed our brief review of the fundamental notions that are prerequisites to a good grasp of the material of this book. In the next chapter we examine the problem of generating, selecting, and verifying tests for faults of combinational and sequential digital circuits.

CHAPTER III

Generation, Selection, and Verification of Tests

Since many of the available techniques of generating, selecting, and verifying sets of tests for digital circuits and systems are impractical for large digital systems such as computers, much of our discussion is aimed at smaller-sized subsystems. We use the term *digital circuit* to convey this distinction.

We first discuss test generation. Assume that a digital circuit and a specific fault of that circuit are given. The problem is to find a test or tests that detect or diagnose the fault. Since the test generation procedures for combinational and sequential circuits are very different, the material is presented in two sections. Section 3.1 deals with combinational circuits, and contains relatively complete, adequate methods. Section 3.2 deals with the more difficult problem of sequential circuits, and the results presented are less satisfactory. We also describe the approach to system diagnosis developed by International Business Machines for the System/360 family of computers. This is included to convey some idea of the issues involved in proceeding from test sets for individual circuits, to a coherent approach for diagnosis of a large digital system. It also illustrates the specialization of general methods to deal with a particular type of circuitry.

Application of the methods of Sections 3.1 and 3.2 will yield a test set for a digital circuit. However, the total number of tests produced for a large digital system could be enormous—conceivably as many as one test per system fault. Hence it is often desirable to select a minimal or near-minimal subset of the tests. Methods for doing this, without unduly compromising completeness or diagnostic resolution, are discussed in Section 3.3.

Finally, it is desirable to verify the completeness and diagnostic resolution of the tests. It is also necessary to generate a mapping from fault identities to symptoms (test results). This mapping forms the basis of the fault dictionaries used by the maintenance personnel to diagnose system faults in the field. Both of these tasks are accomplished by simulating the subject system's behavior in the presence of a fault. A comparative discussion of fault simulation methods is given in Section 3.4.

3.1   Methods of Test Generation—Combinational Circuits

We define the problem as follows. The subject is a combinational digital circuit, which is an interconnected set of logic gates without feedback loops. Any gate may suffer any one of the following types of faults:

Output stuck at logical "0" (s–a–0),
output stuck at logical "1" (s–a–1), or
any input line open (either s–a–0 or s–a–1, depending on the circuit type).

We assume that exactly one fault of the above class has, in fact, occurred. The problem then is to construct a test or a set of tests that detects the fault by utilizing only the normal circuit inputs and outputs. (This excludes redundancy in the logic circuit.)[1]

This section gives a brief historical account, concluding with the *d*-algorithm of Roth (1964, 1966, 1967). For brevity, our approach is intuitive rather than formal—we only wish to give a bird's-eye view of the principal results. This account will serve as a guide to the published literature, which the serious student should consult.

3.1.1 Eldred's Results. R. D. Eldred (1959) wrote the first paper on test generation for combinational circuits. He was developing diagnostic programs for the Datamatic-1000, an early vacuum-tube processor. It used so-called *register realizations* for its logic circuits, as shown in Figure 3.1.

Assume that the registers have been tested (by the obvious method of verifying that each flip-flop can be cycled between its SET and RESET states). Assume further that some means exists for writing arbitrary words into the registers, and for observing register contents. Then the problem reduces to that of finding input vectors to a two-level OR-AND circuit which allow detection of its faults by observation of its outputs.

Eldred noted that the "input-line-open" faults of a three-input OR gate (for example) can be detected by the input vectors

$$(1, 0, 0); (0, 1, 0); (0, 0, 1).$$

(An open input to an OR gate behaves like a s–a–0 input.) Any of these vectors will also detect the output s–a–0 fault. The vector (0, 0, 0) must be

---

[1] Friedman (1967) has pointed out some of the difficulties that may arise when undetectable faults in redundant circuits interact with otherwise detectable faults.

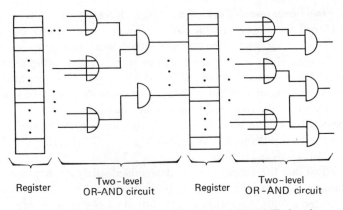

| Register | Two-level OR-AND circuit | Register | Two-level OR-AND circuit |

Figure 3.1 Register realization with two-level OR-AND decoders.

added to the test set to treat the output s–a–1 fault. This approach can be generalized in obvious ways to deal with any type of logic gate and any number of gate inputs. (The test input vectors are close relatives of *primitive d-cubes of a failure*, which we shall encounter in Subsection 3.1.3.)

One difficulty remains. We cannot observe the outputs of the OR gates directly. Instead, we must specify inputs to the second-level ANDs which let us "see" the output of an OR by looking at the AND which it feeds. Stated another way, we must force the OR to "bear the sole responsibility" for determining the output of the AND. The technique for doing so is illustrated in Figure 3.2. Here, input x_3 of the AND controls the AND's output, since the other input values have all been set equal to 1. (This concept can easily be applied to any type of logic gate. It will reappear in more formal dress as the *propagation d-cube*, in Subsection 3.1.3.)

Eldred also noted that the test input vectors often contain "don't cares." These can be used to merge several input vectors, thus creating a single test for several faults.

To sum up: Eldred's work is noteworthy for three reasons. His paper was the first to deal with test generation for combinational circuits. He applied his results to the practical problem of diagnosing the Datamatic-1000. Finally, he was one of the first workers to appreciate the importance of testing a system's hardware, rather than its functions.

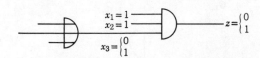

Figure 3.2 Observation of a gate output through another gate.

3.1.2 One-Dimensional Path Sensitizing. Recall that Eldred's results were developed for combinational circuits of one or two levels. *One-dimensional path sensitizing* is an extension of Eldred's work to circuits having any number of levels. Many investigators' names are associated with this method, but none of them seems to have published his work. However, Stieglitz of IBM and Armstrong of Bell Telephone Laboratories are prominently linked with the method in the oral tradition of fault diagnosis.

The basic idea of the method is to choose some path from the site of failure, say gate G_0, through a sequence $G_1, \ldots, G_n$ of gates leading to a circuit output. (This is illustrated in Figure 3.3.) The inputs to $G_1, \ldots, G_n$ are selected so that the output of G_j is determined solely by that input which comes from G_{j-1}, using the technique just described. Thus the output of G_0 can be inferred from observation of the output of G_n. Finally, inputs of G_0 must be specified, to allow the presence or absence of the failure to be inferred from observation of the output of G_0. (This is one of Eldred's ideas, once again.) The path is called a *sensitized path* [the name is attributable to D. B. Armstrong (1966)] and the process just described is called the *forward-trace phase* of the method.

Having set up a sensitized path, we must find a primary input vector that will realize all of the necessary gate input values. This is done by tracing backwards from the inputs of $G_0, \ldots, G_n$ to circuit primary inputs. This obvious extension of Eldred's ideas is known, appropriately enough, as the *backward-trace phase* of the method.

An example will be helpful. Consider the combinational circuit shown in Figure 3.4, and the failure

$$G_7 \text{ output s-a-1.}$$

(For ease of description, we identify the name of a gate with the name of its output signal. Thus

$$G_j = 1$$

Figure 3.3 Selection of a path.

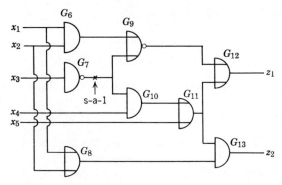

Figure 3.4   Example for one-dimensional path sensitizing.

is to be read as "the output signal of the gate named G_j has value 1.") To begin the forward-trace phase, we select a test that exhibits the failure in terms of inputs and outputs of G_7. This is

$$x_3 = 1.$$

Then

$$G_7 = 0 \quad \text{if the failure is absent,}$$

and

$$G_7 = 1 \quad \text{if the failure is present.}$$

Next we (arbitrarily) choose the path G_7, G_{10}, G_{11}, G_{13} from G_7 to circuit output z_2. The necessary conditions to sensitize this path are

$$x_4 = 1, \quad \text{to sensitize the path through } G_{10},$$
$$x_5 = 0, \quad \text{to sensitize the path through } G_{11},$$

and

$$G_8 = 1.$$

This completes the forward-trace phase for our rather simple example. We now have to find a primary input vector of this circuit that yields all of the conditions laid down thus far—the backward-trace phase. Conveniently enough, the last condition is the only one not already expressed in terms of primary inputs. It may be satisfied by choosing

$$x_1 = 1,$$
$$x_2 = 0.$$

(Notice that this is an arbitrary choice of one of three possibilities.) Thus the backward-trace phase is finished, yielding the input vector

$$\mathbf{X} = (1, 0, 1, 1, 0).$$

When this vector is applied to the circuit,

$$z_2 = 1 \quad \text{if the failure is present,}$$
$$= 0 \quad \text{if the failure is absent.}$$

Also notice that the paths G_7, G_9, G_{12}; and G_7, G_{10}, G_{11}, G_{12} to circuit output z_1 have been (inadvertently) sensitized by the test. However, the failure is not observable at z_1! This is because

$$G_9 = 0, \quad G_{11} = 1 \quad \text{implies} \quad z_1 = 1,$$

if the failure is present; and

$$G_9 = 1, \quad G_{11} = 0 \quad \text{implies} \quad z_1 = 1$$

if the failure is absent. This sort of phenomenon can occur whenever two or more paths fan out from the site of failure and subsequently reconverge, and the parities of inversions along the paths are unequal. *Reconvergent fan-out* has been discussed by Armstrong (1966).

We conclude our discussion of one-dimensional path sensitizing with some general comments.

1. Notice the necessity of making arbitrary choices of gate input signals, as occurred in the example. It can happen that an inappropriate choice may later lead to a conflict in assigned signal values. If this occurs one must "back up," altering any arbitrary choices, until the conflict is resolved. In this event, one is performing a tree search, with all of the well-known difficulties that this implies.

2. The method is *not* an algorithm. A simple counterexample has been provided by Schneider (1967). The circuit is shown in Figure 3.5, and the

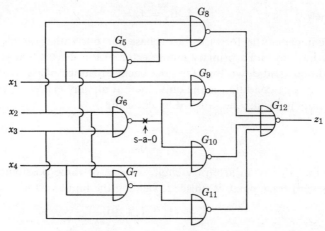

Figure 3.5   Schneider's counterexample.

failure in question is G_6 output s–a–0. It is impossible to generate a test for this failure by strictly adhering to one-dimensional path sensitizing. Any single path must pass through G_9 or G_{10} (but not both). A sensitized path through G_9 and G_{12} requires that

$$G_{10} = 0$$
$$G_{11} = 0.$$

Hence

$$G_7 = 1$$
$$x_4 = 1. \qquad \text{Contradiction.}$$

By symmetry of the circuit, the same argument rules out a path through G_{10} and G_{12}. Hence one-dimensional path sensitizing must fail. And yet, the input vector

$$\mathbf{X} = (0, 0, 0, 0)$$

provides a test for the failure in question.

3. Finally, we must record that the method has proved very useful in practice. When programmed for a digital computer, it is quite economical of storage and running time. In fact, it was used to generate the so-called Fault Locating Tests for the processors of the IBM System/360 family (Hackl and Shirk, 1965). Its major defect lies in its occasional inability to produce a test when one does exist. We now turn to the question of removing this defect.

The reader who studies Schneider's counterexample will soon notice the obvious flaw in the one-dimensional method. It is that only one path is allowed to be sensitized at a time, even in case of reconvergent fanouts with equal inversion parity. The key to an algorithmic method is to sensitize *all possible paths* from the site of failure to the circuit outputs *simultaneously.* This approach has been known informally as *two-dimensional path sensitizing.* It was first formulated precisely by J. Paul Roth (1966, 1967), who christened it the *d-algorithm.*

3.1.3 *The d-Algorithm.* We repeat that the key idea here is to sensitize all possible paths from the site of the fault to all circuit outputs, simultaneously. This concept overcomes the fatal flaw of the one-dimensional method, and therefore leads to an algorithm. Indeed, the *d*-algorithm is the first method for combinational test generation that has been proven to be algorithmic. Roth's formulation is in terms of a mathematical formalism (the calculus of cubical complexes) which many engineers find rather opaque. The purpose of this subsection is to present an abbreviated summary of Roth's main results, intended to serve as an introduction to his (1964, 1966, 1967) papers. You should study these papers for a complete appreciation of Roth's contributions.

The basic procedure of the *d*-algorithm is as follows. First, pick a test for the fault *f* in terms of the inputs and output of the failed gate. Next, generate all possible paths from the site of failure to all circuit outputs, simultaneously. At each step, check for cancellation caused by reconvergent fan out, and abandon the cancelled paths if this occurs. (This step is a generalization of the forward-trace phase of the one-dimensional method; Roth calls it the *d-drive*.) Finally, try to construct a consistent primary input vector which realizes all of the conditions generated during the *d*-drive. This last step is conceptually identical to the backward-trace phase of the one-dimensional method; Roth calls it the *consistency operation*.

Before we can describe the *d*-algorithm in more detail, we must introduce a small amount of new notation and terminology. Like everything else in this subsection, it is taken mostly from Roth's work.[2]

(*a*) *Singular Cover.* Consider the OR gate and the small table shown in Figure 3.6. The table is called the *singular cover* of the gate, and can be considered as a rearranged truth table represented in a compact form. Each row is called a *cube*, and defines a causal relationship between the input and output signals associated with the OR gate. For example, the first cube says that (output) signal number 3 has value 1 if (input) signal number 1 has value 1, regardless of the value of (input) signal number 2. The singular cover representation can be used to describe any logic gate. Also, notice that the singular cover of a combinational circuit is built up from the singular covers of its constituent gates in a simple way. This is illustrated in Figure 3.7. Also notice our naming convention. Each *vertex* of the circuit is assigned an integer label. A gate is given the name of the vertex where its output signal appears. Each vertex therefore corresponds either to a gate output signal or a primary input signal. Finally, we assign vertex numbers by a *levelling rule*. Namely, the integer associated with a gate *G* shall be greater than the integers of all vertices which feed *G*. (This full ordering convention simplifies the consistency operation. It is also related to the rule for *logic organizing*, which is described in Section 4.2.)

(*b*) *Propagation d-Cube.* This imposing term denotes a rather neat notation for expressing one of Eldred's concepts. The concept is that of forcing one gate input to "bear the sole responsibility" for determining the gate's output. The notation is illustrated in Figure 3.8, for the case of a two-input OR gate.

1	2	3
1	*x*	1
x	1	1
0	0	0

Figure 3.6   Gate and singular cover.

[2] Some of this notation is at variance with the notation of the rest of this book. We have chosen to stay with Roth's notation, rather than recast his results in "our" notation, to make it easier for the reader to study Roth's papers. Indeed, one of our prime purposes is to vigorously encourage the reader to study these papers.

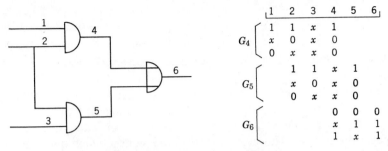

	1	2	3	4	5	6
G_4	1	1	x	1		
	x	0	x	0		
	0	x	x	0		
G_5			1	1	x	1
			x	0	x	0
			0	x	x	0
G_6				0	0	0
				x	1	1
				1	x	1

Figure 3.7   Circuit and singular cover.

Here, d is a symbol that may assume the Boolean values 0 and 1. However, all appearances of d in a cube are constrained to take the same value. Thus d is a kind of constrained "don't care," and the cube

$$\begin{array}{ccc} 1 & 2 & 3 \\ \hline d & 0 & d \end{array}$$

is shorthand for the set

$$\left\{ \begin{array}{ccc} 1 & 2 & 3 \\ \hline 0 & 0 & 0 \end{array} , \quad \begin{array}{ccc} 1 & 2 & 3 \\ \hline 1 & 0 & 1 \end{array} \right\}.$$

This cube expresses the fact that vertex 3 is controlled by vertex 1 when vertex 2 has value 0. Propagation d-cubes can be derived from the singular cover by an algorithm of Roth (1966) or, in simple cases, they can be written down by inspection.[3] Notice that the formalism can be easily generalized to include

---

[3] Roth's algorithm is as follows. To systematically construct propagation d-cubes, we intersect cubes of the gate's singular cover. The cubes must have different output values, and their input values are intersected by these rules:

$$0 \cap 0 = 0 \cap x = x \cap 0 = 0$$
$$1 \cap 1 = 1 \cap x = x \cap 1 = 1$$
$$x \cap x = x$$
$$1 \cap 0 = d, \qquad 0 \cap 1 = d'$$

For example, the singular cover of a two-input OR is

$$\begin{array}{cccc} & 1 & 2 & 3 \\ \hline C1 = & 1 & x & 1 \\ C2 = & x & 1 & 1 \\ C3 = & 0 & 0 & 0 \end{array}$$

The above algorithm yields

$$\begin{array}{cccc} & 1 & 2 & 3 \\ \hline C1 \cap C3 = & d & 0 & d \\ C2 \cap C3 = & 0 & d & d \end{array}$$

as propagation d-cubes of the gate.

$$
\begin{array}{ccc}
1 & 2 & 3 \\
\hline
d & 0 & d \\
0 & d & d
\end{array}
$$

Figure 3.8   Propagation *d*-cubes of a logical block (gate).

the case of several inputs jointly controlling a gate output. Finally, note that Roth calls these cubes "primitive *d*-cubes of a logical block."

(*c*) *Primitive d-Cube of a Failure.* This formalism appears identical to the propagation *d*-cube. However, the two are conceptually quite different animals. Failure to keep this in mind can lead the reader into considerable confusion. The primitive *d*-cube of a failure is used to express tests for a failure in terms of the input and output vertices of the failed gate. An example is shown in Figure 3.9. Here, the OR-gate has suffered an output s–a–1 fault. The corresponding primitive *d*-cube of failure,

$$
\begin{array}{|ccc|}
\hline
1 & 2 & 3 \\
\hline
0 & 0 & d' \\
\end{array}
$$

states that, with vertices 1 and 2 forced to 0, vertex 3 will have value 1 if the fault is present and value 0 if it is absent. Similarly, for a NOR gate, the cube

$$
\begin{array}{|ccc|}
\hline
1 & 2 & 3 \\
\hline
0 & 0 & d \\
\end{array}
$$

says that, with vertices 1 and 2 forced to 0, vertex 3 will have value 0 if some fault is present and value 1 if it is absent.[4]

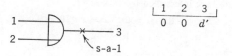

Figure 3.9   Primitive *d*-cube of a failure.

---

[4] Just like the propagation *d*-cubes, primitive *d*-cubes of a failure can usually be written down by inspection. However, Roth has given an algorithm for this step, too. Here is a brief description of the algorithm, which would also be useful in any programmed implementation of the *d*-algorithm.

We construct primitive *d*-cubes of a failure by intersecting pairs of cubes, just as is done for propagation *d*-cubes. We even use the same rules of intersection, as set out above. However, here we select one cube of each pair from the singular cover of the failure-free gate; the other member is the corresponding cube from the singular cover of the failed gate. Assignment of primes is handled by the following convention. A vertex of the intersection has value *d'* if the vertex has value 0 in the cube of the failure-free gate, and value 1 in the cube of the failed gate. The other possibility gets value *d*.

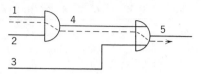

Figure 3.10 Interconnection of gates.

(d) *d-Intersection:* Suppose that we have gates interconnected as in Figure 3.10. We wish to generate a sensitized path from vertex 1 to vertex 5. The relevant propagation *d*-cubes for the two gates are, respectively,

$$C1 = \begin{array}{|ccccc|} 1 & 2 & 3 & 4 & 5 \\ d & 1 & x & d & x \end{array} \quad \text{and} \quad C2 = \begin{array}{|ccccc|} 1 & 2 & 3 & 4 & 5 \\ x & x & 0 & d & d \end{array},$$

the x's being the familiar "don't cares." By inspection, a propagation *d*-cube which represents the sensitized path from vertex 1 to vertex 5 is

$$C3 = \begin{array}{|ccccc|} 1 & 2 & 3 & 4 & 5 \\ d & 1 & 0 & d & d \end{array}.$$

If we wish to define a binary operator $\underset{d}{\cap}$ on $C1$ and $C2$ to yield $C3$, our example suggests that

$$d \underset{d}{\cap} x = d$$
$$1 \underset{d}{\cap} x = 1$$
$$x \underset{d}{\cap} 0 = 0$$
$$d \underset{d}{\cap} d = d$$
$$x \underset{d}{\cap} d = d.$$

Roth's name for $\underset{d}{\cap}$ is *d-intersection*, and the process of computing $C3$ from $C1$ and $C2$ is an example of its use. It is the basic tool for building sensitized paths, and is completely defined by Table 3.1. It is easy to verify that this definition is consistent with our brief example. The symbols ϕ and ψ

Table 3.1 Definition of *d*-Intersection Operator

$\underset{d}{\cap}$	0	1	x	d	d'
0	0	ϕ	0	ψ	ψ
1	ϕ	1	1	ψ	ψ
x	0	1	x	d	d'
d	ψ	ψ	d	μ	λ
d'	ψ	ψ	d'	λ	μ

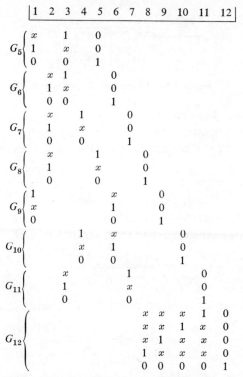

	1	2	3	4	5	6	7	8	9	10	11	12
G_5	x		1		0							
	1		x		0							
	0		0		1							
G_6		x	1			0						
		1	x			0						
		0	0			1						
G_7		x		1			0					
		1		x			0					
		0		0			1					
G_8		x			1			0				
		1			x			0				
		0			0			1				
G_9	1					x			0			
	x					1			0			
	0					0			1			
G_{10}				1		x				0		
				x		1				0		
				0		0				1		
G_{11}		x					1				0	
		1					x				0	
		0					0				1	
G_{12}								x	x	x	1	0
								x	x	1	x	0
								x	1	x	x	0
								1	x	x	x	0
								0	0	0	0	1

Figure 3.11   Singular cover for Schneider's example.

mean that d-intersection is empty and undefined, respectively; the meaning of λ and μ will come clear in the sequel.

Since all of the necessary preliminaries are now in hand, we can discuss the d-algorithm itself. This is best done by an example. We use Schneider's example (Figure 3.5), which was also a counterexample to the one-dimensional method. The singular cover is given in Figure 3.11,[5] and some of the propagation d-cubes are given in Figure 3.12. Recall that these cubes denote the ways in which one or more inputs can be made to control a gate's output. Figure 3.12 gives all cubes that only involve one gate input: the *single d-cubes*. Cubes that denote two or more inputs jointly controlling a gate output— the *double* or *multiple d-cubes*—are generated when required as the algorithm proceeds.

We begin by writing down a primitive d-cube of the failure, vertex 6 s–a–0, which we label test cube 0 (Figure 3.13). We start the process of sensitizing all possible paths from the failure site to circuit outputs by computing the

---

[5] As usual, the portion associated with each gate is set off by a bracket marked with the gate's name. Also note that the symbols " " and "x" are synonymous here.

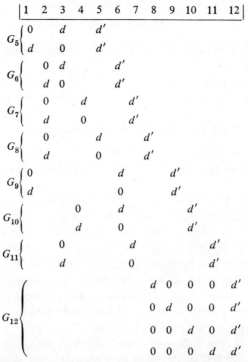

Figure 3.12   Single propagation cubes for Schneider's example.

activity vector of tc^0. Put informally, this specifies the circuit vertices where the fault can be observed. More formally; vertex j is a coordinate of the activity vector $\mathbf{a}(tc)$ of test cube tc iff:

(a) j is a coordinate of tc,
(b) j has value d or d' in tc,

and

(c) j is a primary output of the subcircuit defined by those coordinates of tc whose values are not x.[6]

d-Intersection 1 2 3 4 5 6 7 8 9 10 11 12	Label	Activity	d-Fanout	Comments
0 0 d	tc^0	{6}	{9, 10}	Primitive d-cube of failure

Figure 3.13   First cycle of d-drive.

[6] Here primary outputs are *all* vertices of the subcircuit which feed other gates.

For our example we have

$$\mathbf{a}(tc^0) = \{6\}.$$

[Notice here that vertices 2 and 3 satisfy all conditions, except (b), for inclusion in $\mathbf{a}(tc^0)$.]

Finally, we compute the *d-fanout* of tc^0. This is simply a list of the gates that are "potential extenders" of the paths sensitized thus far. It is computed by finding all gates that are fed by vertices appearing in $\mathbf{a}$. In our example, since vertex 6 feeds gates 9 and 10, the d-fanout of tc^0 is

$$\{9, 10\}.$$

This completes the first cycle of the d-drive (or forward-trace) phase of the algorithm.

The next cycle consists of an attempt to propagate one step further the path(s) sensitized thus far. The essence of the d-algorithm is that we attempt to *simultaneously* propagate *all* sensitized paths—it is this proviso that makes the procedure an algorithm. This might lead the reader to believe that we must intersect every test cube generated to date with every propagation cube of the circuit. However, we are saved from this computationally horrible prospect by two observations: (1) we need only consider propagation cubes of gates that belong to the d-fanout of a test cube (indeed, this is the reason for introducing the notion of d-fanout); and (2) we can, of course, discard all such intersections that do not extend a sensitized path.

In this case, the first observation says that we form d-intersections of tc^0 with the propagation cubes of gates 9 and 10. For gate 9, we have the propagation cubes

$$\begin{array}{|ccc|}\hline 1 & 6 & 9 \\\hline d & 0 & d' \end{array} \quad \text{and} \quad \begin{array}{|ccc|}\hline 1 & 6 & 9 \\\hline 0 & d & d' \end{array}$$

The intersection of tc^0 with the first cube is

$$\begin{array}{|ccccc|}\hline 1 & 2 & 3 & 6 & 9 \\\hline d & 0 & 0 & \psi & d' \end{array}$$

This clearly does not extend the sensitized path; therefore, we discard it.

The intersection of tc^0 with the second cube is

$$\begin{array}{|ccccc|}\hline 1 & 2 & 3 & 6 & 9 \\\hline x & 0 & 0 & d & x \end{array} \overset{\cap}{{}_{d}} \begin{array}{|ccccc|}\hline 1 & 2 & 3 & 6 & 9 \\\hline 0 & x & x & d & d' \end{array} = \begin{array}{|ccccc|}\hline 1 & 2 & 3 & 6 & 9 \\\hline 0 & 0 & 0 & \mu & d' \end{array}$$

What meaning should we give to the symbol μ? Recall that the meaning of the second expression is:

"Vertex 6 controls the output of gate 9 under the specified conditions. Further, the output signal will be the logical complement of the signal supplied at vertex 6."

Hence the intersection is[7]

$$
\begin{array}{|ccccc|}
1 & 2 & 3 & 6 & 9 \\
\hline
0 & 0 & 0 & d & d'
\end{array} \, .
$$

Roth (1966) states all of this formally as part of his definition of d-intersection:

"If only μ (but not λ) occurs in the d-intersection, then for these coordinates let $d \underset{d}{\cap} d = d,\ d' \underset{d}{\cap} d' = d'$."

(Shortly we shall see what happens when λ, the other unexplained symbol in Table 3.1, occurs.)

The propagation cubes of gate 10 lead to a similar result. Hence we get two new test cubes, which we label $tc^{0,1}$ and $tc^{0,2}$ (Figure 3.14). Just as before, we compute the activity vectors and d-fanouts of these cubes. Observe that we are now propagating two distinct paths simultaneously. Also, gates 9 and 10 still appear in the d-fanouts of $tc^{0,1}$ and $tc^{0,2}$ because these gates are fed by gate 6, which is still active.

One more cycle of the d-drive process yields Figure 3.15. Here there are two noteworthy points. First, $tc^{0,1} \underset{d}{\cap} \{12\}$ yields

$$
tc^{0,1} \underset{d}{\cap}
\begin{array}{|ccccc|}
8 & 9 & 10 & 11 & 12 \\
\hline
0 & d & 0 & 0 & d'
\end{array}
$$

$$
=
\begin{array}{|cccccccccccc|}
1 & 2 & 3 & 4 & 5 & 6 & 7 & 8 & 9 & 10 & 11 & 12 \\
\hline
0 & 0 & 0 & x & x & d & x & x & d' & x & x & x
\end{array}
$$

$$
\underset{d}{\cap}
\begin{array}{cccccccccccc}
x & x & x & x & x & x & x & 0 & d & 0 & 0 & d'
\end{array}
$$

$$
=
\begin{array}{|cccccccccccc|}
1 & 2 & 3 & 4 & 5 & 6 & 7 & 8 & 9 & 10 & 11 & 12 \\
\hline
0 & 0 & 0 & x & x & d & x & 0 & \lambda & 0 & 0 & d'
\end{array} \, ,
$$

	d-Intersection		Label	Activity	d-Fanout	Comments
	1 2 3 4 5 6 7 8 9 10 11 12					
tc^0	0 0 d		tc^0	$\{6\}$	$\{9, 10\}$	Primitive d-cube of failure
$tc^0 \underset{d}{\cap} \{9\} =$	0 0 0 d d'		$tc^{0,1}$	$\{6, 9\}$	$\{9, 10, 12\}$	A single path through G_9
$tc^0 \underset{d}{\cap} \{10\} =$	0 0 0 d d'		$tc^{0,2}$	$\{6, 10\}$	$\{9, 10, 12\}$	A single path through G_{10}

Figure 3.14   Second cycle of d-drive.

[7] Henceforth, we shall go through these steps implicitly.

	d-Intersection												Label	Ac-tivity	*d*-Fanout	Comments
	1	2	3	4	5	6	7	8	9	10	11	12				
$tc^{0,1} =$	0	0	0			d			d'						$\{9, 10, 12\}$	Repeated from Figure 3.14
$tc^{0,1} \underset{d}{\cap} \{9\} =$	0	0	0			d			d'							Drop, nothing new
$tc^{0,1} \underset{d}{\cap} \{10\} =$	0	0	0	0		d			d'	d'			$tc^{0,1,1}$	$\{9, 10\}$	$\{12\}$	Two paths through G_9 *and* G_{10}
$tc^{0,1} \underset{d}{\cap} \{12\} =$	0	0	0			d		0	d'	0	0	d	$tc^{0,1,2}$	$\{12\}$	ϕ	Go to consistency test. Also, *d*-fanout is empty, cannot drive forward further

Figure 3.15 Third cycle of *d*-drive.

according to the definition of *d*-intersection set out in Table 3.1. What meaning should we give to the symbol λ? Recall that the meaning of the second factor is:

"Vertex 9 controls the output of gate 12 under the specified conditions. Further, the output signal will be the logical complement of the signal supplied at vertex 9."

Now both

$$\begin{array}{|ccccc|} 8 & 9 & 10 & 11 & 12 \\ \hline 0 & d & 0 & 0 & d' \end{array} \quad \text{and} \quad \begin{array}{|ccccc|} 8 & 9 & 10 & 11 & 12 \\ \hline 0 & d' & 0 & 0 & d \end{array}$$

are symbolic representations of this meaning. Hence they are clearly equivalent, and can be exchanged at will. If we use the second representation, the *d*-intersection becomes

$$\begin{array}{c|cccccccccccc|} & 1 & 2 & 3 & 4 & 5 & 6 & 7 & 8 & 9 & 10 & 11 & 12 \\ \hline & 0 & 0 & 0 & x & x & d & x & x & d' & x & x & x \\ \underset{d}{\cap} & x & x & x & x & x & x & x & 0 & d' & 0 & 0 & d \\ & 1 & 2 & 3 & 4 & 5 & 6 & 7 & 8 & 9 & 10 & 11 & 12 \\ \hline = & 0 & 0 & 0 & x & x & d & x & 0 & \mu & 0 & 0 & d \end{array}$$

which, by the discussion of μ just given, is

$$\begin{array}{|cccccccccccc|} 1 & 2 & 3 & 4 & 5 & 6 & 7 & 8 & 9 & 10 & 11 & 12 \\ \hline 0 & 0 & 0 & x & x & d & x & 0 & d' & 0 & 0 & d \end{array} .$$

Roth (1966) states all of this formally as another part of his definition of d-intersection:

"If only λ (but not μ) occurs, then in the second factor change all those coordinates which are d to d', and those which are d' to d."

Complications arise when both λ and μ occur in an intersection. We would like to take care of the intersections of type λ, namely,

$$d \underset{d}{\cap} d' \quad \text{and} \quad d' \underset{d}{\cap} d,$$

by the method given above. However, the intersections of type μ, namely,

$$d \underset{d}{\cap} d \quad \text{and} \quad d' \underset{d}{\cap} d'$$

would be converted to type λ if this were done. Hence we cannot form a meaningful intersection when λ and μ both occur. Roth states this formally as: "If *both* λ and μ occur, the d-intersection is not defined." This concludes our remarks on the symbols λ and μ.

The other noteworthy point of Figure 3.15 is that the circuit output, vertex 12, appears in the activity vector of $tc^{0,1,2}$. Consequently this cube will be one of the inputs to the backward-trace phase of the algorithm. Also the d-fanout of $tc^{0,1,2}$ is empty; therefore, it cannot be driven forward any further.

The next cycle of the d-drive yields Figure 3.16, which is of no particular interest. The final cycle (Figure 3.17) attempts to propagate $tc^{0,1,1}$ through gate 12. Now coordinates 9 and 10 of $tc^{0,1,1}$ are both inputs to gate 12 and both have value d'. This says that these inputs must jointly determine gate 12's output. Recall that all of the propagation cubes of Figure 3.12 are single d-cubes; that is, they involve only one controlling input. None of these cubes will therefore be of any use here, and indeed all of their d-intersections with

	d-Intersection	Label	Activity	d-Fanout	Comments
	1 2 3 4 5 6 7 8 9 10 11 12				
$tc^{0,2} =$	0 0 0 d d'			$\{9, 10, 12\}$	Repeat from Figure 3.14
$tc^{0,2} \underset{d}{\cap} \{9\} =$	0 0 0 0 d d' d'	$tc^{0,2,1}$			Identical to $tc^{0,1,1}$—Drop
$tc^{0,2} \underset{d}{\cap} \{10\} =$	0 0 0 d d'				Drop, nothing new
$tc^{0,2} \underset{d}{\cap} \{12\} =$	0 0 0 d 0 0 d' 0 d	$tc^{0,2,2}$	$\{12\}$	ϕ	Go to consistency test Also, d-fanout is empty, cannot drive forward further

Figure 3.16 Fourth cycle of d-drive.

	d-Intersection												Label	Activity	d-Fanout	Comments
	1	2	3	4	5	6	7	8	9	10	11	12				
$tc^{0,1,1}$	0	0	0	0		d			d'	d'					{12}	Repeated from Figure 3.15
$tc^{0,1,1} \underset{d}{\cap} \{12\} =$	0	0	0	0		d		0	d'	d'	0	d	$tc^{0,1,1,1}$	{12}	ϕ	No single d-cube of G_{12} works. Go to demand computation of double d-cubes, giving $\lfloor 8\ 9\ 10\ 11\ 12 \rfloor$ $0\ d'\ d'\ 0\ d$. Go to consistency test

Figure 3.17   Last cycle of d-drive.

$tc^{0,1,1}$ are undefined. Hence we must try to generate a propagation cube of gate 12 in which inputs 8 and 9 jointly control the output—a so-called *double d-cube.*

Recourse either to trial and error or to an algorithm of Roth[8] (1966) yields

$$\frac{\lfloor 8 \quad 9 \quad 10 \quad 11 \quad 12 \rfloor}{0 \quad d' \quad d' \quad 0 \quad d}$$

which is just what we require. Using this double d-cube, we get Figure 3.17.

We have now driven all sensitized paths as far forward as possible. It is therefore time to start the back-trace phase of the algorithm. The basic idea of the back-trace phase (or consistency operation) is familiar. We try to work backwards from the vertices of sensitized path(s) to primary inputs, so as to construct a vector of primary input values which will sensitize the path(s).

Let us begin with $tc^{0,1,2}$ (see Figure 3.15). We select the highest-numbered vertex[9] v_j of $tc^{0,1,2}$ which has value 1 or 0. (In this case, it is vertex 11.) Next we find a cube of the singular cover (from Figure 3.11) which has v_j as output vertex, bearing the same value as in $tc^{0,1,2}$. d-Intersecting this cube with $tc^{0,1,2}$ in effect specifies input values to the gate whose output vertex is v_j. Hence the first four lines of Figure 3.18. We repeat this process for the other vertices, always working in descending numerical order. This yields the balance of Figure 3.18, which shows that there exists no test corresponding

[8] Double or multiple d-cubes are generally formed by successive intersections of cubes in the singular cover. For example, the cube $\dfrac{\lfloor 8\ 9\ 10\ 11\ 12 \rfloor}{0\ d'\ d'\ 0\ d}$ of gate 12 can be generated by intersecting cube (0 0 0 0 1) with cubes (x x 1 x 0) and (x 1 x x 0). (See Figure 3.11.)

[9] Recall that vertex numbers were assigned so that any gate output vertex has a higher number than all vertices which feed it. This convention facilitates the consistency operation.

	d-Intersection												Label	Activity	d-Fanout	Comments
	1	2	3	4	5	6	7	8	9	10	11	12				
$tc^{0,1,2} =$	0	0	0			d	0	d'	0	0		d				Start with $tc^{0,1,2}$. Vertex 11 must be 0. From Figure 3.11, there are two possibilities. $G_{11}(b)$ conflicts. Choose $G_{11}(a)$.
$G_{11}(a) =$				x		1										
$G_{11}(b) =$				1		x										
$tc^{0,1,2} \cap_d G_{11}(a) \cap_d G_{10}(a) =$	0	0	0			d	1	0	d'	0	0	d				Vertex 10 must be 0. There are two possibilities. $G_{10}(b)$ conflicts. Choose $G_{10}(a)$.
$G_{10}(a) =$					1			x								
$G_{10}(b) =$					x			1								
$tc^{0,1,2} \cap_d G_{11}(a) \cap_d G_{10}(a) =$	0	0	1			d	1	0	d'	0	0	d				Vertex 8 must be 0. There are two possibilities. $G_8(a)$ conflicts. Choose $G_8(b)$.
$G_8(a) =$			1				x									
$G_8(b) =$			x				1									
$tc^{0,1,2} \cap_d G_{11}(a) \cap_d G_{10}(a) \cap_d G_8(b) =$	0	0	0	1	d	1	0	d'	0	0		d				Vertex 7 must be 1. There is only one choice, and it conflicts. Hence there exists no test corresponding to $tc^{0,1,2}$.
$G_7(a) =$	0	0		1												

Figure 3.18 Consistency operation for $tc^{0,1,2}$.

	$d\bar{\;}$-intersection												Label	Activity	d-Fanout	Comments
	1	2	3	4	5	6	7	8	9	10	11	12				
$tc^{0.1.1.1}$ =	0	0	0	0		d	0		d'		0	d				Start with $tc^{0.1.1.1}$. Vertex 11 must be 0. There are two possibilities.
$G_{11}(a)$ =			x			1										$G_{11}(b)$ conflicts. Choose $G_{11}(a)$.
$G_{11}(b)$ =			1			x										
$tc^{0.1.1.1} \underset{d}{\cap} G_{11}(a) \underset{d}{\cap} G_{11}(a)$ =	0	0	0	0		d	1	0	d'	d'	0	d				Vertex 8 must be 0. There are two possibilities. $G_8(a)$ conflicts. Choose $G_8(b)$.
$G_8(a)$ =				x			0									
$G_8(b)$ =				x		1	0									
$tc^{0.1.1.1} \underset{d}{\cap} G_{11}(a) \underset{d}{\cap} G_8(b)$ =	0	0	0	0	1	d	1	0	d'	d'	0	d				Vertex 7 must be 1
$G_7(a)$ =					0	0	1									Only one choice
$tc^{0.1.1.1} \underset{d}{\cap} G_{11}(a) \underset{d}{\cap} G_8(b) \underset{d}{\cap} G_7(a)$ =	0	0	0	0	1	d	1	0	d'	d'	0	d				Vertex 5 must be 1
$G_5(a)$ =					0	0	1									Only one choice
Valid test →	0	0	0	0	1	d	1	0	d'	d'	0	d				All conditions have been checked for consistency. $tc^{0.1.1.1}$ therefore produces one test, namely, $\mathbf{x} = (0, 0, 0, 0)$.

Figure 3.19 Consistency operation for $tc^{0.1.1.1}$.

to $tc^{0,1,2}$. You may try the process for $tc^{0,2,2}$ and obtain the same result. Figure 3.19 documents the consistency operation applied to $tc^{0,1,1,1}$, and yields the single input vector

$$(\mathbf{X}) = (0, 0, 0, 0).$$

This concludes our example illustrating the mechanics of the d-algorithm. We now turn to Roth's theorem, which establishes that the method is an algorithm. The following material is not completely self-contained; it is intended only as an introduction to the proof given in Roth (1966). Alternately, you may skip this discussion with little loss of continuity.

Roth has proved the following theorem: If there exists a test T for some failure f of a combinational network (circuit) N, then the d-algorithm will compute a test cube $C(\hat{T}, f)$ where $\hat{T}$ is a cube which contains[10] T. We give a brief outline of the method of proof, illustrating it with our example.

The proof hinges on a quantity C^*. We show that

    (1) C^* defines a set of tests T^* which contains T,

and

    (2) the d-algorithm computes C^*.

To define C^* easily, we first introduce some notation. Let $N^1, \ldots, N^r$ be a set of cubes. Then the d-intersection of these cubes is written

$$\partial(N) \triangleq N^1 \underset{d}{\cap} N^2 \underset{d}{\cap} \cdots \underset{d}{\cap} N^r.$$

Now we can define C^* in terms of its components, namely:

$$C^* \triangleq \alpha^0 \underset{d}{\cap} \partial(\alpha) \underset{d}{\cap} \partial(\beta) \underset{d}{\cap} \partial(\gamma).$$

These components will now be discussed separately.

    (a) Let α^0 be a primitive d-cube of the failure f.

Hence, for our example, the fault

"vertex 6 s–a–0"

is represented by

1	2	3	4	5	6	7	8	9	10	11	12
x	0	0	x	x	d	x	x	x	x	x	x

$\alpha^0 \triangleq$

---

[10] In the usual sense of switching theory, namely, a cube $\mathbf{U} = (U_1, U_2, \ldots, U_n)$ is said to contain $\mathbf{V} = (V_1, V_2, \ldots, V_n)$ if $V_i = U_i \cap V_i$, for all i.

(b) Let I be a gate not the site of failure, and having a d or d' output coordinate in $C(T, f)$. Define the jth bit of a d-cube α^I by

$$\alpha_j^I \triangleq C(T, f)_j \quad \text{for inputs and outputs of gate } I;$$
$$\triangleq x \quad \text{otherwise.}$$

In our example,

	1	2	3	4	5	6	7	8	9	10	11	12
$C(T, f) =$	0	0	0	0	1	d	1	0	d'	d'	0	d ;

α^I is defined for gates 9, 10, and 12, and

	1	2	3	4	5	6	7	8	9	10	11	12
$\alpha^9 =$	0	x	x	x	x	d	x	x	d'	x	x	x
$\alpha^{10} =$	x	x	x	0	x	d	x	x	x	d'	x	x
$\alpha^{12} =$	x	x	x	x	x	x	x	0	d'	d'	0	d

Hence

	1	2	3	4	5	6	7	8	9	10	11	12
$\partial(\alpha) =$	0	x	x	0	x	d	x	0	d'	d'	0	d .

(c) Let J be a gate whose output in $C(T, f)$ is 1 or 0, and whose inputs do not have value d or d' in $C(T, f)$. Define the rth bit of a cube β^J by

$$\beta_r^J \triangleq C(T, f)_r \quad \text{if} \quad C(T, f)_r \in \{0, 1\}$$
$$\triangleq x \quad \text{if} \quad C(T, f)_r \in \{x, d, d'\}$$

for r running over coordinates of gate J, and

$$\beta_r^J \triangleq x \quad \text{everywhere else.}$$

In our example, β^J is defined only for gates 5, 7, 8, and 11. [These are the only gates whose outputs in $C(T, f)$ are 1 or 0, and whose inputs in $C(T, f)$ are not d or d'.] We have

	1	2	3	4	5	6	7	8	9	10	11	12
$\beta^5 =$	0	x	0	x	1	x	x	x	x	x	x	x
$\beta^7 =$	x	0	x	0	x	x	1	x	x	x	x	x
$\beta^8 =$	x	0	x	x	1	x	x	0	x	x	x	x
$\beta^{11} =$	x	x	0	x	x	x	1	x	x	x	0	x

Hence

$$\partial(\beta) = 0 \quad 0 \quad 0 \quad 0 \quad 1 \quad x \quad 1 \quad 0 \quad x \quad x \quad 0 \quad x.$$

(d) Let K be a logic gate whose output in $C(T, f)$ is 1 or 0, and which has both d and d' as input values. Define the pth bit of γ^K by

$$\gamma_p^K \triangleq C(T, f)_p \qquad \text{for} \qquad p = K$$
$$\triangleq x \qquad\qquad \text{everywhere else.}$$

Our example has no such gates, so that

$$\partial(\gamma) = \phi.$$

With the above definitions, we have partitioned the gates of a circuit into four classes, namely:

(a) the failed gate—the α^0 class;
(b) the gates which do not lie in any sensitized path—the β class;
(c) the gates which do lie in some sensitized path(s)—the α and γ classes, for which
(d) the gates at which two or more sensitized paths reconverge and cancel each other comprise the γ class. (An instance of this phenomenon was pointed out in the example of Figure 3.4.)

Roth first proves that C^* defines a set of tests $\hat{T}$ for f. We verify this result for our example by computing

$$C^* = \alpha^0 \underset{d}{\cap} \partial(\alpha) \underset{d}{\cap} \partial(\beta) \underset{d}{\cap} \partial(\gamma)$$

	1	2	3	4	5	6	7	8	9	10	11	12	
$=$	x	0	0	x	x	d	x	x	x	x	x	x	$[\alpha^0]$
$\underset{d}{\cap}$	0	x	x	0	x	d	x	0	d'	d'	0	d	$[\partial(\alpha)]$
$\underset{d}{\cap}$	0	0	0	0	1	x	1	0	x	x	0	x	$[\partial(\beta)]$
$=$	0	0	0	0	1	d	1	0	d'	d'	0	d	

which shows that

1	2	3	4
0	0	0	0

is a test for the fault "vertex 6 s–a–0."

The second part of the proof requires that we show that C^* is computed by the d-algorithm. Our working of the example has, in fact, verified this claim in the case of the example. The details of the proof are beyond the scope of this treatment. However, we hope that this material will help the reader in his study of Roth's theorem.

We conclude our discussion of the d-algorithm with a few opinions about its significance. From the theoretical viewpoint, it represents the culmination of a chain of investigation reaching back to Eldred's early work. Being algorithmic, it is the first completely satisfactory solution to the problem of test generation in combinational circuits. From the practical viewpoint, let us make two observations. First, we cannot yet pass judgment on its value as a useful computational scheme. The only implementation we know of was done by interpretively executing a program written in Iverson's (1966) APL language. The results were reported by Roth (1967), but they are inconclusive because of the inefficiencies of interpretively executing APL code. However, we believe that a more efficient implementation would yield running time and storage requirements comparable to the one-dimensional method.

Finally, notice that the problem that we have discussed is a simplification of the problem usually encountered in practice. Instead of one specific fault of a circuit, we are usually given a *class* of faults for which tests must be devised. Now we can always use the *d*-algorithm to generate one test for each fault, and simply concatenate the tests. However, the test set generated by this method for a digital processor could easily have more than 10^5 members —far too many to store and use economically. Moreover, this naïve approach fails to exploit the full powers of the *d*-algorithm, because a test generated by the *d*-algorithm for a particular fault generally detects many other faults as well. This point is illustrated by the example just discussed, where the test input vector

$$\mathbf{X} = (0, 0, 0, 0)$$

was generated for the fault

vertex 6 s–a–0.

However, this test also serves to detect the faults

vertex 9 s–a–1

vertex 10 s–a–1

and

vertex 12 s–a–0.

This observation suggests a general approach to the problem of reducing the size of test sets. We could use the *d*-algorithm to generate a test for a particular fault, and then examine the resulting sensitized path(s), for example by Roth's (1967) program TEST DETECT. Any fault that "lies on" such a path and that causes the path signal to change value will also be detected. A second general approach, the equivalent normal form method of Armstrong, is discussed next. Additional approaches, based on tabular methods, are discussed in Section 3.3. Finally, notice that a basic requirement here is that we identify the total set of faults which a given test, in fact, detects. Methods of *fault simulation*, which provide systematic ways of doing this identification, are discussed in Section 3.4.

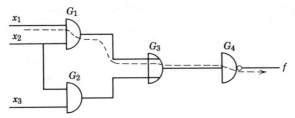

Figure 3.20   Example for enf method.

3.1.4   The Equivalent Normal Form.

We have just mentioned the practical problem of finding a fairly small set of tests, which will diagnose a circuit subject to a large number of faults. Most of our discussion of this problem is in Section 3.3. Here, we discuss a method of test generation which is well suited to the selection of *efficient* (near-minimal) test sets. This method, known as the *enf* (equivalent normal form) method is due to D. B. Armstrong (1966).

The enf of a single-output, combinational circuit is constructed as follows.

(a) Write down the Boolean expression realized by the circuit. Corresponding to each gate G_j of the circuit, there shall be a pair of parentheses in the expression, the parentheses being labelled with the symbol j. The subexpression corresponding to G_j shall be enclosed in the parentheses. Furthermore, all literals in the Boolean expression will denote input variables of the circuit.

(b) Expand to sum-of-products normal form. When a pair of parentheses is removed, its associated label is attached to each literal inside the parentheses, as a subscript. No redundant terms are removed.

As an example, consider the combinational circuit of Figure 3.20, for which

$$f = [((x1 \cdot x2)_1 \vee (x2 \cdot x3)_2)_3]'_4.$$

Expanding,

$$f = [(x1_1 \cdot x2_1 \vee x2_2 \cdot x3_2)_3]'_4$$
$$= (x1_{13} \cdot x2_{13} \vee x2_{23} \cdot x3_{23})'_4$$
$$= (x1_{134} \cdot x2_{134})' \cdot (x2_{234} \cdot x3_{234})'$$
$$= (x1'_{134} \vee x2'_{134}) \cdot (x2'_{234} \vee x3'_{234})$$
$$= x1'_{134} \cdot x2'_{234} \vee x2'_{134} \cdot x2'_{234}$$
$$\vee x1'_{134} \cdot x3'_{234} \vee x2'_{134} \cdot x3'_{234},$$

this last expression being the enf. Observe that each literal appearance corresponds to a path from some circuit input to the circuit output, the path being specified by the string of subscripts. These observations lead to the following theorem of Armstrong's:

"A test for a literal appearance in the enf sensitizes the corresponding path in the circuit. Thus, if a set of literal appearances can be selected whose corresponding paths together contain every vertex of the circuit, and if a set of tests can be found which tests at least one appearance of each literal for the s–a–1 and s–a–0 faults, then the set of tests detects every fault of the circuit."

For example,

$$x1' = 0, \qquad x2' = 0, \qquad x3' = 1$$

provides a test for the s–a–1 fault of the appearance of literal $x1'_{134}$, in the third term of the enf. The theorem then tells us that this input vector sensitizes the path marked in Figure 3.20. Now we have observed (in connection with the *d*-algorithm) that certain other faults "lying in" a sensitized path will be detected. That remark holds true here; the faults

$$G_1 \quad \text{s–a–0}$$
$$G_3 \quad \text{s–a–0}$$

and

$$G_4 \quad \text{s–a–1}$$

will also be detected. Moreover, our test is also a test for the literal appearance $x2'_{134}$ in the fourth term of the enf. Hence a second path has inadvertently been sensitized, and the fault

$$x2 \text{ (input to } G_1) \text{ s–a–0}$$

will also be detected.

Is the enf method an algorithm? Armstrong conjectures in his paper that it is, and we concur. However, to prove that the method is algorithmic, we must show that the sets of literals and tests mentioned in the theorem do, in fact, always exist. This question is still unsettled—as far as we know, neither a proof nor a counterexample has been found.

To conclude, we make several comments about the significance of this work. Armstrong's 1966 paper was the first to formally put forward the notion of sensitized path. Second, the enf method will sensitize multiple paths, as you may verify by trying it on Schneider's example of Figure 3.5. It is therefore a more powerful method than one-dimensional path sensitizing. Third, the enf method can be programmed for a computer, but the number of literal appearances becomes unmanageable for the larger circuits encountered in practice.

Finally, we saw in the example that a test generated for a given fault may detect many additional faults. Moreover, the additional faults can be identified easily; thus we have the nucleus of a procedure to reduce the size of a test set. (All of this is literally a repetition of remarks made in connection with the Roth *d*-algorithm. See the closing lines of Subsection 3.1.3.) Armstrong has enlarged on this point, and the details can be found in his 1966 paper.

3.1.5 Poage's Results.   In his doctoral thesis, J. F. Poage (1963) made several contributions to the test generation problem. Although his results are generally impractical for the large circuits often encountered in practice, they are remarkably thorough and complete. He gave methods for generating a minimal set of tests to detect all single and multiple faults of a combinational circuit and for finding the set of single and multiple faults detected by a given test. This work was done for both gate and contact (i.e., relay) circuits; we shall discuss only gate circuits here. Moreover, he considered the problem of test generation for sequential circuits—we describe those results in Section 3.2.

A key part of Poage's work is the development of a sort of calculus for faults. He has given a symbolic method for computing the functions realized by a circuit with failures. The development is as follows. For any wire *j* of the circuit, we define associated Boolean variables called *fault parameters*:

$$j_0 : j_0 = 1 \quad \text{iff wire } j \text{ is s--a--0}$$
$$j_1 : j_1 = 1 \quad \text{iff wire } j \text{ is s--a--1}$$
$$j_n : j_n = 1 \quad \text{iff wire } j \text{ is failure-free (normal).}$$

Then, if the signal carried by wire *j* realizes the Boolean variable *w*, we may replace the literal *w* by

$$w^* = w \cdot j_n \vee j_1.$$

This expresses necessary and sufficient conditions for the signal on wire *j* to have value 1; that is,

$$w = 1 \quad \text{and} \quad j \text{ is failure-free,}$$

or

$$j \text{ is s--a--1.}$$

The analogous formulation for the signal on wire *j* to have value 0 is

$$w^{*\prime} = w' \cdot j_n \vee j_0$$

which also follows from

$$(w^*)' = (w \cdot j_n \vee j_1)'$$
$$= (w' \vee j_n') \cdot (j_1')$$
$$= (w' \vee j_0 \vee j_1)(j_n \vee j_0)$$
$$= w' \cdot j_n \vee j_0$$

where, because of the three-state nature of the fault parameters, $j_n' = j_0 \vee j_1$; $j_n \cdot j_1 = j_n \cdot j_0 = j_0 \cdot j_1 = 0$; etc.

If we carry out this substitution for all wires $a, b, c, \ldots$ of a circuit realizing some function f of input variables $x_1, \ldots, x_m$,

$$f(x_1, \ldots, x_m)$$

becomes

$$f^*(x_1, \ldots, x_m; a_0, b_0, \ldots; a_1, b_1, \ldots; a_n, b_n, \ldots)$$

By assigning appropriate nonconflicting values to the fault parameters we can obtain the circuit output function corresponding to any single or multiple fault from f^*. For example,

$$j_0 = 1, \qquad j_1 = 0, \qquad j_n = 0 \qquad \text{for wire } j$$
$$k_0 = 0, \qquad k_1 = 0, \qquad k_n = 1 \qquad \text{for all wires } k \neq j$$

is the value assignment corresponding to the single fault

"wire j is s–a–0."

This formulation is therefore a symbolic analogue of the methods of fault simulation discussed in Section 3.4.

We now study the correspondence between f and f^*, on the one hand, and f' and $f^{*\prime}$, on the other hand. Consider the trivial circuit of Figure 3.21. We have $f = x \cdot y$, and the output has value 1 when f^* is true:

$$
\begin{aligned}
f^* &= (x^* \cdot y^*) \cdot 3_n \vee 3_1 \\
&= (((x \cdot 1_n \vee 1_1) \cdot (y \cdot 2_n \vee 2_1)) \cdot 3_n \vee 3_1) \\
&= [(x \cdot 1_n \vee 1_1) \cdot 3_n \vee 3_1] \cdot [(y \cdot 2_n \vee 2_1) \cdot 3_n \vee 3_1]
\end{aligned}
$$

The expressions in square brackets, each containing a single input literal, are called *literal propositions*. Poage has proved the theorem that functions realized by a combinational circuit can always be written in terms of literal propositions.

The nested structure of fault parameters in each literal proposition makes it possible to use the compact notation

$$f^* = x(1_1, 3_1) \cdot y(2_1, 3_1).$$

Observe that the forms of f and f^* are now identical, with the literal propositions of f^* replacing literals of f. Notice further that information about the structure of the circuit (that is, the paths from input to output and all faults on them) appears in the literal propositions. Analogous relationships hold true for

Figure 3.21   Example showing correspondence of f and $f.^*$

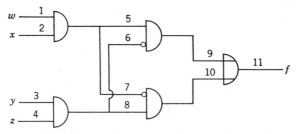

Figure 3.22   Example for Poage's method—combinational circuits.

the complementary output function. We have $f' = x' \vee y'$, and the output has value 0 when $f*'$ is true:

$$f*' = (x* \cdot y*)' \cdot 3_n \vee 3_0$$
$$= x'(1_0, 3_0) \vee y'(2_0, 3_0),$$

since

$$x*' = (x \cdot 1_n \vee 1_1)' = x' \cdot 1_n \vee 1_0 = x'(1_0).$$

This example also illustrates the property that the complement of a literal proposition is obtained by complementing the input literal and changing the subscript of the fault parameters from 1 to 0 or vice versa.

In general, the output functions $f*$ and $f*'$ may be developed from either the inputs or the output. For the circuit of Figure 3.22, we get

$$f* = f(11_1) = 9*(11_1) \vee 10*(11_1)$$
$$= 5*(9_1, 11_1) \cdot 6*'(9_1, 11_1) \vee 7*'(10_1, 11_1) \cdot 8*(10_1, 11_1)$$

etc.

or

$$1* = w(1_1)$$
$$5* = 1*(5_1) \cdot 2*(5_1) = w(1_1, 5_1) \cdot x(2_1, 5_1)$$
$$6* = y(3_1, 6_1) \cdot z(4_1, 6_1)$$
$$9* = 5*(9_1) \cdot 6*'(9_1)$$
$$= w(1_1, 5_1, 9_1) \cdot x(2_1, 5_1, 9_1) \cdot [y'(3_0, 6_0, 9_1) \vee z'(4_0, 6_0, 9_1)].$$

Finally,

$$f* = w(1_1, 5_1, 9_1, 11_1) \cdot x(2_1, 5_1, 9_1, 11_1) \cdot y'(3_0, 6_0, 9_1, 11_1)$$
$$\vee\ w(1_1, 5_1, 9_1, 11_1) \cdot x(2_1, 5_1, 9_1, 11_1) \cdot z'(4_0, 6_0, 9_1, 11_1)$$
$$\vee\ y(3_1, 8_1, 10_1, 11_1) \cdot z(4_1, 8_1, 10_1, 11_1) \cdot w'(1_0, 7_0, 10_1, 11_1)$$
$$\vee\ y(3_1, 8_1, 10_1, 11_1) \cdot z(4_1, 8_1, 10_1, 11_1) \cdot x'(2_0, 7_0, 10_1, 11_1),$$

where, again, literal propositions correspond to literals of the fault-free function

$$f = wxy' \vee wxz' \vee yzw' \vee yzx'.$$

The complementary output function $f^{*'}$ can be derived similarly from the circuit, or by complementing f^*. Thus,

$$
\begin{aligned}
f^{*'} = \; & [w'(1_0, 5_0, 9_0, 11_0) \lor x'(2_0, 5_0, 9_0, 11_0) \lor y(3_1, 6_1, 9_0, 11_0)] \\
& \cdot [w'(1_0, 5_0, 9_0, 11_0) \lor x'(2_0, 5_0, 9_0, 11_0) \lor z(4_1, 6_1, 9_0, 11_0)] \\
& \cdot [y'(3_0, 8_0, 10_0, 11_0) \lor z'(4_0, 8_0, 10_0, 11_0) \lor w(1_1, 7_1, 10_0, 11_0)] \\
& \cdot [y'(3_0, 8_0, 10_0, 11_0) \lor z'(4_0, 8_0, 10_0, 11_0) \lor x(2_1, 7_1, 10_0, 11_0)].
\end{aligned}
$$

This function, when converted to sum-of-products form, includes terms such as

$$
w'(1_0, 5_0, 9_0, 11_0) \cdot w(1_1, 7_1, 10_0, 11_0) \cdot x(2_1, 7_1, 10_0, 11_0)
$$

whose counterpart $w'wx$ would normally have been eliminated from the fault-free function f' because $w'w = 0$. Here, however, the literal propositions corresponding to the literals w' and w are *not* complements. Thus, the correspondence between $f^{*'}$ and f' is maintained only if f' is written as

$$
f' = [w' \lor x' \lor y] \cdot [w' \lor x' \lor z] \cdot [y' \lor z' \lor w] \cdot [y' \lor z' \lor x]
$$

or

$$
f' = wxyz \lor w'y' \lor w'z' \lor x'y' \lor x'z' \lor w'wx \lor x'wx \lor yzy' \lor yzz'.
$$

It is easily verified that f^* and $f^{*'}$ reduce to the appropriate singly or multiply "failed" functions when specific values are assigned to the fault parameters. Note, however, that fault parameters are associated with gate inputs in this example. Therefore, an output fault on a gate having fanout must be represented as a multiple fault; for example, the single fault "output of gate $w \cdot x$ stuck-at-1 is specified by $5_1, 7_1$. On the other hand, this formulation allows us to consider individual input faults on lines 5 and 7.

Another strong similarity, which the reader may have noticed, exists between f^* and the enf of Armstrong. Specifically, the path information required by the enf method can be obtained from the normal-form representation of f^* by a trivial change of notation. For our example,

$$
f_{\text{enf}} = w_{1,5,9,11} x_{2,5,9,11} y'_{3,6,9,11} \lor w_{1,5,9,11} x_{2,5,9,11} z'_{4,6,9,11} \lor y_{3,8,10,11} z_{4,8,10,11} w'_{1,7,10,11}
$$
$$
\lor y_{3,8,10,11} z_{4,8,10,11} x'_{2,7,10,11}.
$$

(The similarity between f^* and f_{enf} would have been even more obvious if fault parameters had been associated with gate outputs rather than gate inputs.) A comparison of f_{enf} and f^* suggests that Poage anticipated Armstrong's enf formulation. However, Poage uses the f^* formalism in a manner very unlike Armstrong's use of the enf. This will be born out by the following account.

The problem considered is the construction of a fault table for a combinational circuit. Recall (from Section 2.3) that a fault table is a rectangular binary array having one row for each admissible fault and one column for each input vector which can be applied to the circuit.[11] The (i, j)th entry of the table is 1 iff the jth input vector detects the ith fault. Poage argues that in some cases of interest the table will have many more rows than columns. (This would be true, for example, if multiple faults were considered and if the circuit inputs were only indirectly accessible, through other logic.) In such cases it is clearly best to construct the fault table column by column. To do this, we must be able to compute the set of all faults detected by a given test. We now consider this subproblem.

We illustrate Poage's approach with another of our ubiquitous small examples. Consider the circuit of Figure 3.22, the set of faults included in the sum-of-products representation given just above,[12] and the input vector

$$(w, x, y, z) = (0, 0, 0, 1).$$

Now $f(0, 0, 0, 1) = 0$. Hence the faults detected by this test will be just those which cause the output to change from 0 to 1, when they are inserted into the circuit. Such faults must make one or more terms of the sum-of-products representation of f^* assume value 1; for example, consider the first term,

$$w(1_1, 5_1, 9_1, 11_1) \cdot x(2_1, 5_1, 9_1, 11_1) \cdot y(3_0, 6_0, 9_1 \ 11_1).$$

The first two literal propositions have value 0 in the failure-free circuit, and the last has value 1. We seek all nonconflicting values of the fault parameters which cause the first two propositions to assume value 1, as well as preserving the value of the last proposition. Now for $(w, x, y, z) = (0, 0, 0, 1)$, the literal propositions in expanded form are

$$((((w \cdot 1_n \vee 1_1) \cdot 5_n \vee 5_1) \cdot 9_n \vee 9_1) \cdot 11_n \vee 11_1)|_{w=0},$$

$$((((x \cdot 2_n \vee 2_1) \cdot 5_n \vee 5_1) \cdot 9_n \vee 9_1) \cdot 11_n \vee 11_1)|_{x=0},$$

and

$$((((y' \cdot 3_n \vee 3_0) \cdot 6_n \vee 6_0) \cdot 9_n \vee 9_1) \cdot 11_n \vee 11_1)|_{y=0}.$$

These become

$$11_1 \vee 9_1 \cdot 11_n \vee 5_1 \cdot 9_n \cdot 11_n \vee 1_1 \cdot 5_n \cdot 9_n \cdot 11_n,$$

$$11_1 \vee 9_1 \cdot 11_n \vee 5_1 \cdot 9_n \cdot 11_n \vee 2_1 \cdot 5_n \cdot 9_n \cdot 11_n,$$

and

$$11_1 \vee 9_1 \cdot 11_n \vee 6_0 \cdot 9_n \cdot 11_n \vee 3_0 \cdot 6_n \cdot 9_n \cdot 11_n \vee 3_n \cdot 6_n \cdot 9_n \cdot 11_n.$$

Each of these Boolean expressions explicitly denotes the set of faults which

---

[11] The fault table is the raw material from which the various *fault dictionaries* are made. See Chapter 5.

[12] Notice that this set of faults is incomplete. The procedure must be repeated, using $f^{*\prime}$ to treat remaining faults, or setting $j_1 = j_n = 0$ to obtain $j_0 = 1$.

will assign it value 1. The intersection of these faults is of course the set which assigns value 1 to the term. Finally, the union of sets so derived over the four terms of f^* is the set of faults detected by the given test.

We do not write out the intersection explicitly; it would be tiresome to do so even for our small example. Indeed, even the representation set out above is unwieldy. We can achieve economy of space by writing

$$w(1_1, 5_1, 9_1, 11_1)|_{w=0} \triangleq 11_1 \vee 9_1 \cdot 11_n \vee 5_1 \cdot 9_n \cdot 11_n \vee 1_1 \cdot 5_n \cdot 9_n \cdot 11_n$$

$$x(2_1, 5_1, 9_1, 11_1)|_{x=0} \triangleq 11_1 \vee 9_1 \cdot 11_n \vee 5_1 \cdot 9_n \cdot 11_n \vee 2_1 \cdot 5_n \cdot 9_n \cdot 11_n$$

$$y'(3_0, 6_0, 9_1, 11_1)|_{y'=1} \triangleq 11_1 \vee 9_1 \cdot 11_n \vee 6_0 \cdot 9_n \cdot 11_n \vee 3_0 \cdot 6_n \cdot 9_n \cdot 11_n$$

$$\vee \, 3_n \cdot 6_n \cdot 9_n \cdot 11_n.$$

Thus the intersection of fault sets can be compactly written as

$$w(1_1, 5_1, 9_1, 11_1)|_{w=0} \cdot x(2_1, 5_1, 9_1, 11_1)|_{x=0} \cdot y'(3_0, 6_0, 9_1, 11_1)|_{y'=1}$$

This concludes our discussion on computation of the set of faults detected by a given test. Poage (1963) has shown how to specialize these results to treat single faults only.

Once the fault table has been constructed by the above technique, one may ask for a minimal subset of the tests which detects all faults. Poage has observed that this problem is precisely equivalent to the classical minimal cover problem of switching theory. Hence all of the techniques available for the latter problem (e.g., the Quine-McCluskey method), may be directly applied to the former. Poage also gives techniques for simplifying the fault table, before subjecting it to a minimization procedure.

To summarize, Poage has given a complete, satisfying treatment of the fault detection problem for small combinational circuits. However, the computation required would be excessive in the case of large circuits (say, in excess of 100 gates) even with the aid of a computer. The problem of dealing with such circuits, which are not unknown in digital processors, will be considered in Section 3.4. In addition, the problem of *test existence* has been avoided. We have tacitly assumed that a specified fault can be detected by at least one of the permissible input vectors. This problem, in turn, touches on the issues of redundancy and incomplete test sets, which we shall discuss later.

3.1.6 Summary. We have followed the mainstream of research in combinational test generation, from Eldred's first contributions to the present. We have not considered the problem of test generation for faults of sequential circuits, nor have we fully dealt with the problem of selecting an efficient test set for all faults of a circuit. We return to the latter problem in Section 3.3; the former problem is our next topic.

3.2 Methods of Test Generation—Sequential Circuits

We have mentioned that test generation is a difficult problem for sequential circuits; much more so than for combinational circuits. One approach to the problem is formal—we attempt to develop algorithms, just as was done for combinational circuits. This approach has not been very successful for any but the simplest sequential circuits because of the following difficulties. First, each candidate test input must usually be evaluated for each possible circuit state. Hence the amount of computation required to evaluate a test doubles for each memory element in the circuit. Second, there is the problem of initialization. Before we can apply a test to a sequential circuit, we must be able to force it into a fixed, known state; or, at the very least, we must know what state it is in. This may be done by preceding the first test with a *homing sequence*. Homing sequences have been studied by Hennie (1964). They may be very lengthy, and they may not exist for some sequential circuits. Alternatively, we must provide special reset circuitry capable of doing the same job. Either method must be valid both for the fault-free circuit and for all of the failed circuits. In the case of reset circuitry, this includes failures of the reset circuitry itself! Moreover, if combinational testing is to be used, every test must begin either with a homing sequence or with operation of the reset circuitry. For all of these reasons, algorithmic methods have not been particularly successful in dealing with large sequential systems.

A second approach involves physically opening the feedback lines of the subject when testing is performed, thereby making it combinational. This approach has shown promise for synchronous circuits (after all, the clock signal is supposed to do just this); but difficulties emerge in connection with asynchronous circuits. Specifically, any critical races or oscillations introduced under failure will be missed when the tests are evaluated.

Finally, heuristic methods have been developed to deal with sequential circuits. These methods can be used to treat fairly large circuits (i.e., a good-sized fraction of a digital processor), and they can be applied to synchronous or asynchronous circuits. However, they are by no means guaranteed to produce optimal test sequences. Indeed, they may not even produce a complete test sequence.

In this section we first describe some work by Poage and McCluskey (1964), as a representative example of the algorithmic approach to test generation.[13] Next we describe four heuristics due to Seshu (1965), to illustrate the heuristic approach. We conclude with a description of the techniques that have been developed to handle a special class of very large sequential systems—the processors of the IBM System/360 family of computers.

---

[13] Other notable papers that take this general approach have been written by Hennie (1964), Kime (1966), and Kohavi and Lavallée (1967a, 1967b).

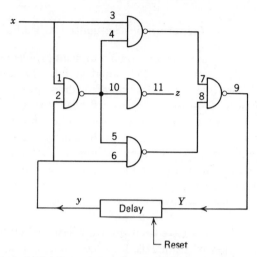

Figure 3.23 Example for Poage's method—sequential circuits.

3.2.1 Poage's Results. The problem that Poage and McCluskey (1964) considered was the derivation of a shortest test sequence, to perform fault detection for a sequential circuit. The subject is described by a *flow table*[14] (which immediately puts a practical limit on the complexity that the subject can have). Flow tables are also derived for all possible failed machines. The procedure involves the combination of this set of flow tables into a composite table, which is used to find an optimal test sequence. The method is essentially an extension of Poage's results for combinational circuits (see Subsection 3.1.5). Feedback loops are conceptually opened to make the subject combinational, and failure parameters are included in the Boolean equations written down for the combinational circuit. Since the subject is assumed to be deterministic and synchronous, races and oscillations are of no interest. The number of internal states (some may be not accessible) is assumed to be fixed (i.e., insertion of a failure does not create any new memory). It is also assumed that a reset facility is provided, and that failures are solid and logical.

The procedure is perhaps best illustrated by an example. Consider the sequential circuit of Figure 3.23, and let the set of permissible single faults be

$$\{2_1, 3_1, 4_1, 5_0\}.$$

(Here 2_1, for example, means line 2 s–a–1.) The expressions for the feedback

---

[14] See Huffman (1954) or any textbook on sequential machine theory for a definition of flow table.

Table 3.2   Boolean Expressions for Failed Circuits

Fault	Machine Number	Y	z
No fault	M_1	$xy' \vee x'y$	xy
2_1 (Wire 2 s–a–1)	M_2	$x'y$	x
3_1 (Wire 3 s–a–1)	M_3	$x' \vee y'$	xy
4_1 (Wire 4 s–a–1)	M_4	$x \vee y$	xy
5_0 (Wire 5 s–a–0)	M_5	xy'	xy

and primary outputs, expressed in terms of Poage's literal propositions, are

$$Y^* = x(3_1, 7_0, 9_1) \cdot [x'(1_0, 4_1, 7_0, 9_1) \vee y'(2_0, 4_1, 7_0, 9_1)]$$
$$\vee\, y(6_1, 8_0, 9_1) \cdot [x'(1_0, 5_1, 8_0, 9_1) \vee y'(2_0, 5_1, 8_0, 9_1)]$$
$$z^* = x(1_1, 10_0, 11_1) \cdot y(2_1, 10_0, 11_1)$$

Recall that these expressions reduce to the expressions for the circuit under failure, when appropriate values are assigned to the fault parameters. The results are shown in Table 3.2.[15] The flow tables that result from these expressions are shown in Figure 3.24. The reset state is always shown in the first row by convention.

M_1 (Good machine)

T_1	$x = 0$	$x = 1$
0	0/0	1/0
y		
1	1/0	0/1

M_2 (Wire 2   s–a–1)

T_2	$x = 0$	$x = 1$
0	0/0	0/1
y		
1	1/0	0/1

M_3 (Wire 3   s–a–1)

T_3	$x = 0$	$x = 1$
0	1/0	1/0
y		
1	1/0	0/1

M_4 (Wire 4   s–a–1)

T_4	$x = 0$	$x = 1$
0	0/0	1/0
y		
1	1/0	1/1

M_5 (Wire 5   s–a–0)

T_5	$x = 0$	$x = 1$
0	0/0	1/0
y		
1	0/0	0/1

Notation: each entry represents next state/primary output.
Figure   3.24   Flow Tables.

[15] We can use the expressions for Y^* and z^* to derive the failed expressions for 2_1 and 5_0. Alternately, setting $2_0 = 0$, $2_n = 0$ gives the expression for 2_1. Similarly, for 5_0.

Now the goal of Poage's procedure is to find an optimal (shortest) test sequence to distinguish between the good machine and any of the failed machines. To see how this is done, consider machine M_2. To distinguish M_2 from M_1, we obviously need to find a sequence of input vectors which, starting with M_1 and M_2 in the common reset state, causes M_2 to produce an output sequence differing at some point from M_1's. The sequence

$$(R), (1)$$

does the trick,[16] the outputs being

$$(0) \quad \text{for} \quad M_1$$

and

$$(1) \quad \text{for} \quad M_2.$$

In the same vein, you can verify that the sequence

$$(R), (1), (0), (1)$$

serves to distinguish M_5 from M_1.

To formalize this process, we define the *product table* of flow tables T_i and T_j as follows. If the entry of T_i at coordinates $(\mathbf{y}_s, \mathbf{X}_k)_i$ is $\mathbf{Y}_t/\mathbf{Z}_t$, and if the entry of T_j at coordinates $(\mathbf{y}_p, \mathbf{X}_k)_j$ is $\mathbf{Y}_q/\mathbf{Z}_q$; then the entry of the product table $T_i \times T_j$ at coordinates $(\mathbf{y}_s\mathbf{y}_p, \mathbf{X}_k)_{i \times j}$ is $\mathbf{Y}_t\mathbf{Y}_q/\mathbf{Z}_t\mathbf{Z}_q$. Thus $T_i \times T_j$ is just the flow table of the parallel connection of the machines which realize T_i and T_j.

As an illustration, we compute $T_1 \times T_5$. From the reset product state

$$y_1y_5 = 00,$$

both primary input values lead to product states whose primary output components agree. Hence we must go further to find a distinguishing sequence for M_1 and M_5. From the state

$$y_1y_5 = 11,$$

input value

$$\mathbf{X} = (0)$$

leads to product state $10/00$. That is, M_1 enters state

$$\mathbf{Y} = (1)$$

whereas M_5 enters state

$$\mathbf{Y} = (0).$$

However, the outputs of M_1 and M_5 still agree; therefore, we must analyze product state 10 further. Under the input

$$\mathbf{X} = (1),$$

---

[16] R denotes the action of operating the reset circuitry. In the sequel, we assume that each test sequence discussed will include R unless otherwise stated explicitly.

$T_1 \times T_2$	$x = 0$	$x = 1$
0 0	00/00	10/ (01)

P_{12}

$T_1 \times T_3$	$x = 0$	$x = 1$
0 0	01/00	11/00
0 1	01/00	10/ (01)
1 1	11/00	00/11

P_{13}

$T_1 \times T_4$	$x = 0$	$x = 1$
0 0	00/00	11/00
1 1	11/00	01/11
0 1	01/00	11/ (01)

P_{14}

$T_1 \times T_5$	$x = 0$	$x = 1$
0 0	00/00	11/00
1 1	10/00	00/11
1 0	10/00	01/ (10)

P_{15}

Figure 3.25   Product tables.

the product state 10 leads to entry 01/10. Hence the primary outputs of M_1 and M_5 finally disagree. The table is completed by forming a new row $y_1 y_5$ for each new entry $Y_1 Y_5$ which appears, if the corresponding outputs agree. The final result is shown in Figure 3.25.

Now the purpose of forming a product flow table is to derive a sequence of inputs, beginning at the reset point, which distinguishes the pair of machines in question. We can therefore simplify the product table somewhat, since only the primary outputs that differ are of interest here. We do this by marking the entries at which outputs differ with an asterisk; all other outputs are omitted and the states are represented by convenient symbols. Simplified product tables for the tables of Figure 3.25 are given in Figure 3.26. Of course, we could have written the simplified product tables directly from the original tables of Figure 3.24. If we had done so, it would have been easier to find

$T_1 \times T_2$	$x = 0$	$x = 1$
A	A	*

P_{12}

$T_1 \times T_3$	$x = 0$	$x = 1$
A	B	C
B	B	*
C	C	A

P_{13}

$T_1 \times T_4$	$x = 0$	$x = 1$
A	A	B
B	B	C
C	C	*

P_{14}

$T_1 \times T_5$	$x = 0$	$x = 1$
A	A	B
B	C	A
C	C	*

P_{15}

Figure 3.26   Simplified product tables.

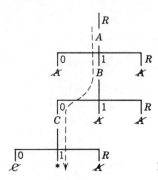

Figure 3.27 Tree representation for a product table.

the distinguishing sequence for M_1 and M_5; we would only have had to find a sequence that sent the product machine into the fault-detecting state "*".

The derivation of distinguishing sequences can be done more systematically with the help of a tree representation for the product table. The tree shows the state-transitions effected by each input for each present state. The tree representation for $T_1 \times T_5$ is shown in Figure 3.27, and the shortest distinguishing sequence is easy to see. Also note that the tree has been pruned in an obvious way, i.e., only the new states are pursued.

We can repeat the analysis just done on M_1 and M_5 to find optimal sequences to distinguish M_1 from M_2, M_3, and M_4. The concatenation of these sequences would provide a fault detection test for the four faults, but it would not necessarily be of minimum length. To find an optimal sequence to detect *all* faults, Poage forms the *product* of the *product tables*. He calls this "product of products" the *sequential fault table*, since it represents the sequences which detect each fault.

For our example, each entry of the sequential fault table is an ordered 4-tuple of product states. (See Figure 3.28.) We start, as before, with the 4-tuple reset state $AAAA$, and follow transitions to new 4-tuple states until no new 4-tuples are generated. There is the important proviso that an asterisk is treated as a "don't care" state, and the successor state to "*" is always "*". This simply expresses the fact that a fault has been detected as soon as the

P_{12}	P_{13}	P_{14}	P_{15}	$x = 0$				$x = 1$			
A	A	A	A	A	B	A	A	*	C	B	B
A	B	A	A	A	B	A	A	*	*	B	B
*	C	B	B	*	C	B	C	*	A	C	A
*	C	B	C	*	C	B	C	*	A	C	*
*	A	C	A	*	B	C	A	*	C	*	B
*	B	C	A	*	B	C	A	*	*	*	B

Figure 3.28 Sequential fault table.

					P_{12}	P_{13}	P_{14}	P_{15}
	A	A	A	A				
	A	B	A	A				
x = 0	*	C	B	B	*			
	*	C	B	C	*			
	*	A	C	A	*			
	*	B	C	A	*			
	A	A	A	A	*			
	A	B	A	A	*	*		
x = 1	*	C	B	B	*			
	*	C	B	C	*			*
	*	A	C	A	*		*	
	*	B	C	A	*	*	*	

Figure 3.29   Rewritten sequential fault table.

corresponding component of the 4-tuple state assumes the value *. The behavior resulting from the fault is therefore of no interest from that point onward. Thus, stated in terms of the sequential fault table, our task is to find an optimal input sequence which starts at state $AAAA$, and causes each component of the 4-tuple state to assume the value * at least once.

Just as before, we can find such a sequence either by trial and error, or by representing the sequential fault table as a tree. However, there is one trick that can be usefully applied before the tree representation is made. If we rewrite the sequential fault table of Figure 3.28 in the form of Figure 3.29, it is apparent that any sequence that distinguishes M_5 must involve the 4-tuple state $*CBC$. But $*CBC$ itself provides detection for M_2. Thus M_2 need not be considered further. We can regard this as a covering process in the sense of switching theory. In fact, all of the algorithms available to treat prime implicant tables can be invoked here.

The result of simplifying our sequential fault table by such methods is shown in Figure 3.30. From this, we can find an optimal sequence to detect any of the four faults, namely,

$$(R), (0), (1), (0), (1), (1).$$

P_{13}	P_{14}	P_{15}	x = 0			x = 1		
A	A	A	B	A	A	C	B	B
B	A	A	B	A	A	*	B	B
C	B	B	C	B	C	A	C	A
C	B	C	C	B	C	A	C	*
A	C	A	B	C	A	C	*	B
B	C	A	B	C	A	*	*	B

Figure 3.30   Simplified sequential fault table.

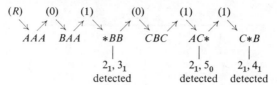

Figure 3.31   Optimal fault detection sequence.

as shown in Figure 3.31. Alternately, we could first represent the simplified sequential fault table as the tree of Figure 3.32. Again, it is pruned as it is developed by abandoning all state 4-tuples which have occurred on the same or a previous level, since they could not lead to a shorter sequence. The sequence can be read off easily from this tree. If the tree had not been pruned, the alternate optimal sequence (R), (1), (0), (1), (0), (1) would have been found.

The step-by-step development given here was chosen mainly for clarity of exposition; in practice we would compute the sequential fault table directly from the tables $T_1, \ldots, T_m$. No other shortcuts appear to be possible. It is possible to relax the restriction that the machine can be reset to a unique state even under failure. However, this would involve consideration of all possible resets produced under failure. An extension of the method to handle fault location is even more awkward.

To summarize, Poage's method is elegant in concept and remarkable in that it produces optimal test sequences. However, it is quite clearly

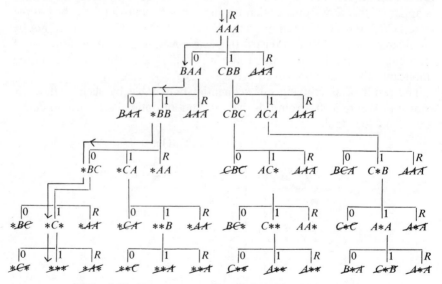

Figure 3.32   Tree representation of the sequential fault table.

impractical for all but small circuits and small classes of faults. We now examine another approach to test generation which has rather complementary characteristics.

3.2.2 Seshu's Heuristics.

We have just noted that Poage's algorithm provides a good test generation method for small sequential circuits. However, it is impractical for large ones. Thus we are forced to rely on less satisfactory methods when we attempt to treat computers or large pieces of computers.

One alternative approach is to use heuristics that are relatively simple, and economical of computer time. We now describe a set of four such heuristics [from Seshu (1965)], which are used by the Sequential Analyzer[17] system of programs to automatically generate tests. In order to fully understand these heuristics, we first must know something about the way in which they interact with their environment, the Sequential Analyzer. An heuristic is presented with a (simulated) sequential circuit plus a specified set of faults. It is asked to propose one or more plausible test inputs to distinguish the faults from each other. These candidate tests are then simulated to determine their performance, and some sort of numerical measure of performance is computed for each. The test input having the highest "figure of merit" is then used, provided that its figure exceeds a threshold value.[18] Otherwise, the heuristic is considered to have failed, and another heuristic is tried. Normally, control passes among the heuristics until a complete test sequence for the sequential circuit has been created. However, if all four heuristics fail, the system gives up. We can now describe the heuristics themselves.

(a) BEST NEXT OR RETURN TO GOOD. This heuristic is based on a sort of continuity assumption. Generally, we assume that small excursions in the primary input space of the subject (measured perhaps by Hamming distance) give rise to only small excursions in state space. Ignoring obvious mathematical difficulties, then, we postulate that the next-state function is a "continuous" function of the primary input vectors. It then seems reasonable that a candidate test which was found to be useful at the jth step of a test sequence is likely to remain useful at step $j + k$, for small values of k. This argument gives rise to the following heuristic procedure. To generate the jth test input for a sequential circuit, first compute all input vectors differing in one bit from the $j - 1$st input. (Remember that successive inputs to an asynchronous circuit are allowed to differ in only one bit.) Evaluate each of

---

[17] The Sequential Analyzer is described in Chapter IV. However, Seshu's heuristics are a method of test generation for sequential circuits; therefore, it is appropriate to describe them here.

[18] Several figures of merit for evaluating the efficiency of tests will be discussed in Section 3.3.

these "next" candidate tests by simulating it and computing its figure of merit. Discard all "next" tests whose figures of merit fall below the threshold. Of the remaining candidates, use the one of greatest figure of merit and put the others on a pushdown list of "good" test inputs. If none of the "next" candidates has an acceptable figure of merit, try the "good" test inputs generated previously. If the pushdown stack is exhausted without finding an acceptable test, the heuristic fails.

Clearly, this heuristic is most effective when the underlying "continuity" assumption is valid. This assumption, in turn, is supported by the asynchronous restriction, which rules out large excursions in the subject's primary input space. Consequently, the heuristic is likely to be ineffective for treating circuits which do not obey the asynchronous restriction. Hence it is not well-suited to treating synchronous logic. Also note that we usually must generate an interpolation sequence tor each a test input taken from the pushdown stack, again because of the asynchronous restriction.

(b) WANDER. This is a very simple heuristic employing a well-known idea. We wander one step from the $j - $ 1st test input by generating all inputs differing in one bit from it. If none of these candidates is acceptable, we change bits cyclically until an input which does not cause any critical races or oscillations is found. We then wander one step from this input. The process continues until a useful test input is found or until the number of steps of wandering exceeds a user-supplied limit. In the latter case the heuristic fails.

(c) RESET. Before we describe this heuristic we must supply a little background information. We test a sequential circuit by applying a sequence of primary input vectors. We then examine the final state of the circuit in order to gain knowledge about the presence or absence of failures. If this approach is to be at all useful, we obviously must know something about the initial state of the circuit from which testing began. We gain this knowledge by assuming the existence of *permissible reset states* having the following properties.

1. A *permissible reset state* (prs) is a primary input state plus a feedback state.

2. It is possible to *momentarily* reset the subject machine's primary and feedback input lines to the values specified by a prs, even under failure.

3. A prs is not necessarily a stable state of any failed machine. However, when the feedback lines are released, a failed machine must eventually enter a stable state without exhibiting misbehavior (critical races or oscillations).

Now we can describe the RESET heuristic. It simply consists of applying the permissible reset states supplied by the user in turn, and selecting the one having the highest figure of merit. Hence a test sequence produced with the aid of the RESET heuristic might require the tester to operate the subject's RESET button several times during testing.

(d) COMBINATIONAL. Here, we conceptually open the feedback lines of the simulated subject, thus rendering it combinational. We then generate a test for each fault by one of the methods of Section 3.1 (by simple one-dimensional path sensitizing, in the present Sequential Analyzer). As soon as a test for some fault is found that does not cause misbehavior, we use it. Thus we apply a test for some fault, generated on the assumption of broken feedback lines, to the subject circuit with unbroken feedback lines. The hope here, then, is that the action of the unbroken feedback loops will not compromise the test too much. As the reader may suspect, this heuristic is most effective with *sparsely sequential* circuits—circuits having a very low ratio of feedback loops to gates.

This concludes our description of Seshu's heuristics. Their interconnection with the rest of the Sequential Analyzer to form a system for fault simulation and test generation is described in Chapter IV. However, the point we make here is that the BEST NEXT OR RETURN strategy has proved to be most effective in practice. This may result partially from the rather inefficient implementation of the COMBINATIONAL strategy. One should generate several tests for each fault and exploit "don't cares" by merging tests to create a single test for many faults. "Don't cares" should also be employed to minimize feedback dependence of tests. Finally, the procedure uses one-dimensional path sensitizing, which has become obsolete with the advent of two-dimensional methods.

3.2.2 *Special Techniques for the System/360 Processors.* In this section we describe the maintenance scheme used for some of the processors of International Business Machines' System/360 family of computers. The reader is cautioned that these techniques vary widely from model to model of the family, and from machine to machine in the production of a given model. We are attempting to summarize the techniques applied to the System/360 Model 50 processor, as of late 1965. Our material is taken from Hackl and Shirk (1965), and from Carter et al. (1964).

Ease of fault diagnosis was obviously considered carefully during the design of Model 50, which alone is sufficient to set it apart from most general-purpose processors. Special hardware for testing purposes only was included in the design. Some of this hardware is used to provide an extremely complete facility, both to reset the processor to a specified state, and to record its state. This facility is invoked by executing either of two machine functions, which we may call Scan-In and Scan-Out. Execution of Scan-Out causes the state of every memory element (independent feedback loop) in the processor to be recorded in a special, fixed area of core memory. Scan-In is the inverse function; the data found in the special area of memory are used to force the processor into a fixed state. This facility is very powerful and useful. For example, an execution of Scan-Out when a malfunction is first detected will save the entire processor state, for later analysis by program or by the maintenance man. Furthermore, the processor can subsequently be forced back into this state by executing a Scan-In. Finally, the designer of diagnostic tests can put the subject into any convenient state before doing a test by simply writing the appropriate data into the special area of core memory, and then doing a Scan-In function. This vastly simplifies the practical problem of applying desired test stimuli to a given portion of the processor.

Some of the other special hardware is used to allow the processor to be run in small increments. This allows one to perform a small part of an instruction cycle, and then to analyze the results under program control. Hence one gets much better diagnostic resolution than would result if entire instructions had to be executed before the results could be examined.

Finally, Model 50 uses a clean, modularized design. Much of the processor is composed of registers or combinational circuits.[19] (A read-only memory is used for control.) This avoids many difficulties in test generation and fault simulation. For example, one can derive tests for a decoder in terms of its own inputs and outputs, and can rely on the scan functions in order to apply test inputs and observe outputs. In other processors, it is often necessary to consider a much larger piece of the subject when tests are generated. This, in turn, raises the cost of developing the diagnosis procedures.

The process of detecting and diagnosing faults in the field proceeds as follows. The tests were previously derived by one-dimensional path sensitizing, using an IBM 7090. They are stored on a reel of tape, and are read into the Model 50's memory. This is done under control of special, simple control circuits that use ring counters. These are simple enough to allow manual diagnosis by the maintenance man, if they fail. The Scan-In function is then invoked to reset the processor to an initial state. The processor is permitted to advance through a few clock cycles. Next, a Scan-Out is done, and the test results thus obtained are compared with prestored values, by program. The next test is then selected on the basis of this comparison (sequential testing). If a fault is detected, enough diagnostic tests are applied to diagnose it, hopefully to within a few replaceable circuit packages.

Since the tests are produced from a coded description of the Model 50 (the so-called Design Automation File), and since each test is derived by simulating only a small piece of the processor, it is possible to update the procedures when design changes are made to the processor. The *hard core*, or fraction of the processor which must be operable for testing to proceed, is approximately 10 percent of the processor. As the only other entity that

---

[19] Hence much of the logic resembles the register realization shown in Figure 3.1. The scan hardware would consist of special gating paths allowing one to read from or write into any of the registers.

takes part in testing is a human being, it seems fair to call this a self-diagnosis procedure. We suggest that the reader compare this approach to self-diagnosis with the one described in Subsection 4.4.2.

We have now completed our discussions of test generation for combinational and sequential circuits. Application of these procedures, however, may yield a very large set of tests. Therefore, we now examine the problem of reducing the size of the test set without unduly compromising completeness or diagnostic resolution.

3.3 Methods for Test Minimization

We have discussed a number of test generation methods in the previous two sections. These methods allow us to find tests to detect or diagnose faults of combinational and sequential circuits. But an unsolved problem remains. In practice, we often wish to design a test set that will deal with *all* faults of a digital system such as a processor. However, many of our test generation methods produce tests only for a *single, specific* fault. Others treat entire classes of faults at a blow, but cannot be used to treat a subject of processor size. The obvious answer in either case is to apply some method repeatedly, until all of the subject's faults have been treated; and then simply concatenate the resulting tests. This answer may be adequate from an academic viewpoint, but it fails miserably in practice. The test set so created would be of overwhelming size, and hence unacceptable both in required storage and running time. Indeed, in the worst case, it might approach one test per system fault![20] Hence we need methods for reducing the size of a set of tests.

Here we discuss several such methods. Some produce absolutely minimal test sets; others serve to drastically reduce the number of tests without necessarily achieving a true minimum.[21] In either case, the overriding goal is to reduce the number of tests without compromising completeness or diagnostic resolution.

3.3.1 Methods for Selecting Efficient Combinational Procedures. We have already observed that a *fault table* can be used to represent the results of test generation. A fault table is a two-dimensional array having one row for each permissible fault, and one column for each test.[22] For any entry f_{ij} of the

---

[20] Maling and Allen (1963) have suggested that the number of tests may grow roughly linearly with the number of gates, for large combinational circuits. (This is when a certain amount of minimization is done.) The situation is even worse, of course, when the subject has feedback loops.

[21] We use the word "efficient" to cover both cases.

[22] Notice that a fault table is a simplified representation of the simulation data.

table,

$$f_{ij} = 1$$

if the *i*th fault is detected by the *j*th test, and

$$f_{ij} = 0 \qquad \text{otherwise.}$$

The rows of the table are called *fault signatures* or *fault patterns*. Each such pattern is a row vector, hence

$$\mathbf{f}_i = (f_{i1}, f_{i2}, \ldots, f_{im})$$

represents the signature of the *i*th fault. Two fault patterns $\mathbf{f}_i$ and $\mathbf{f}_j$ are *distinguishable* if

$$f_{ik} \neq f_{jk} \qquad \text{for some } k.$$

The problem of finding a minimal test set to detect all faults is one of finding a minimal set of columns of the table so that each row of this subarray has at least one 1. To distinguish all faults from each other and from the good machine, we need a minimal set of columns which satisfies the above, and which also has all rows distinguishable from one another. The obvious approach to both of these problems is exhaustive enumeration; but this is impossibly lengthy for even the smallest nontrivial circuits. More promising approaches are provided by the following:

1. The prime implicant method.
2. The method of test set intersection.
3. The method of distinguishability criteria.

We first discuss the *prime implicant method*. Many people[23] have observed that the problem of finding a minimal test set for *detection* is exactly analogous to the minimal cover problem of switching theory. The analogy is made by simply associating tests with prime implicants and faults with fundamental products. Any of the solutions to the minimal cover problem[24] can then be used directly to find a minimal test set for fault detection.

We can also make an analogy between the minimal cover problem and the problem of finding a minimal set of *diagnostic tests*. This extension is due to Poage (1963), and begins with the construction of a so-called *difference table*. The difference table is constructed from the original fault table. It has all of the rows of the original table, plus a new row for each *pair* of faults of the original table. Each new row is formed by taking the bit-by-bit exclusive-OR of a pair of row vectors from the original table. The 1-entries of these new rows therefore denote tests that serve to distinguish pairs of failed circuits;

[23] For example, Kautz (1967), Poage (1963), and Roth and Wagner (1959).
[24] Most notably, the Quine-McCluskey algorithm. See McCluskey (1956).

the 1-entries of the original rows can now be thought of as tests that distinguish pairs of circuits, of which one is always the failure-free circuit. The Quine-McCluskey method can be directly applied to the difference table to obtain a minimal set of tests.

Although this approach is neat in concept, it is too lengthy for most circuits of practical interest. The difference table for a circuit with n faults has

$$\binom{n}{2} + n = \binom{n+1}{2}$$

rows. Thus, the difference table for a circuit of only twelve gates, having five faults per gate, would have 1830 rows! Hence the usefulness of this approach is very limited.

The second possibility is the *method of test set intersection*. This method is due to Galey, Norby, and Roth (1964). The basic idea is to "preprocess" the simulation data in order to obtain a reduced fault table. The reduced table can then be used directly to form a dictionary, or it can first be minimized by the prime implicant method. The method of test set intersection frequently gives an efficient set of tests; however, it is not guaranteed to produce a minimal set.

The method is as follows. Consider the 1-entries of row vector $\mathbf{f}_1$ in the fault table. They specify the subset of tests which detect fault $\mathbf{f}_1$. We intersect $\mathbf{f}_1$ with $\mathbf{f}_2$ by performing a bit-by-bit AND of these vectors. If

$$\mathbf{f}_1 \cdot \mathbf{f}_2 \neq 0,$$

then the 1-entries of $\mathbf{f}_1 \cdot \mathbf{f}_2$ denote all tests that detect both faults. We replace both $\mathbf{f}_1$ and $\mathbf{f}_2$ with their intersection, and proceed to intersect $\mathbf{f}_1 \cdot \mathbf{f}_2$ with $\mathbf{f}_3$.

On the other hand, if

$$\mathbf{f}_1 \cdot \mathbf{f}_2 = 0,$$

we intersect $\mathbf{f}_1$ with $\mathbf{f}_3$. As before, if

$$\mathbf{f}_1 \cdot \mathbf{f}_3 \neq 0$$

we replace both vectors with their intersection and carry on. But, if

$$\mathbf{f}_1 \cdot \mathbf{f}_3 = 0,$$

we try to intersect $\mathbf{f}_2$ and $\mathbf{f}_3$ next. This process is carried on until all row vectors of the table have been considered. The final result is a reduced fault table. In this table, the 1-entries of a row

$$\mathbf{f}_{i1} \cdot \mathbf{f}_{i2} \cdot \ldots \cdot \mathbf{f}_{ip}$$

denote tests that detect all of faults $f_{i1}, \ldots, f_{ip}$. We can get a set of detection tests from this reduced table either by selecting one representative of each row or by applying the prime implicant method to the reduced table.

An example may clarify this procedure. Consider the fault table of Table

Table 3.3 Fault Table for
Test Set Intersection

	T_1	T_2	T_3	T_4	T_5
f_1	1	1	0	1	0
f_2	1	1	1	0	1
f_3	0	1	1	1	1
f_4	0	1	0	0	1
f_5	0	0	0	1	1
f_6	1	0	1	0	0

3.3, which has six faults and five tests. If we intersect row vectors in the order f_1, f_2, f_3, f_4, f_5, and f_6, we get the reduced table of Table 3.4, and a test set can be formed by selecting one member from each of the groups

$$(T_2);   (T_4, T_5);   (T_1, T_3).$$

However, if we had chosen the order f_2, f_3, f_4, f_5, f_6 and f_1, we could have formed an even smaller set of detection tests, namely, T_1 and T_5. Thus the outcome of this process is very much dependent on the order of intersection. Hence we cannot be sure of getting a minimal test set unless we exhaustively try all possible orders of intersection.

The third method for selecting an efficient test set is the *method of distinguishability criteria*, due to Chang (1965). The method assumes that either a complete or partial (certain columns missing) fault table is available. The basic idea of the method is to assign *weights* to tests. The weights reflect the relative ability of the tests to distinguish faults—hence the name "distinguishability criteria." Tests are systematically selected on the basis of their weights in order to yield an efficient test set. The weight W_j of a test T_j is defined as the number of pairs of faults which it distinguishes. We have

$$W_j = (n_0{}^j) \cdot (n_1{}^j),$$

where $n_0{}^j$ and $n_1{}^j$ are, respectively, the numbers of zeroes and ones in the jth column of the fault table. This measure is compatible with the information gain measure[25] described in Subsection 3.3.2.

The method is organized as a sequence of iterations. First, we compute W_j

Table 3.4 Reduced Fault Table

	T_1	T_2	T_3	T_4	T_5
(f_1, f_2, f_3, f_4)	0	1	0	0	0
f_5	0	0	0	1	1
f_6	1	0	1	0	0

[25] Proposed by Johnson (1960) and Mandelbaum (1964).

for all values of j. We select the test for which W_j is greatest as the first test, since this test distinguishes the greatest number of pairs of faults. Now this first test obviously partitions the faults into two blocks: those that it detects and those that it does not detect. In general, when the ith test has been chosen, the faults will have been partitioned into some number m of disjoint blocks $b_1, \ldots, b_m$. This means that subsequent tests must be chosen in a slightly more complicated way. Let test T_j be one of the candidates for selection as the $(i + 1)$st member of the set, and let

$$(n_0{}^j)_{b_k}$$

and

$$(n_1{}^j)_{b_k}$$

be the numbers of zeroes and ones in block b_k and the jth column of the table. Then the weight for T_j after the ith step of test selection is

$$W_j{}^i = \sum_{k=1}^{m} (n_0{}^j)_{b_k} \cdot (n_1{}^j)_{b_k} \qquad (3.1)$$

The test for which $W_j{}^i$ is maximized is chosen as the $(i + 1)$st member of the test set. The selection of tests is continued in this way until the partition of faults can be refined no further; that is, until the weights of all unused tests are zero.

This method admits of an extension that should be valuable in the near future. This is the ability to select tests that diagnose faults to specified degrees of diagnostic resolution. We have already noted (in Subsection 2.1.3) that the degree of diagnostic resolution that is best for a given subject depends on the quantity of circuitry contained in each replaceable package. As Large Scale Integration becomes more popular, it will be increasingly desirable to have test sets that identify faults only to within one LSI package. We can extend the method of distinguishability criteria in this direction as follows. Suppose, for example, that faults f_1 and f_2 are associated with circuit package p_1; f_3, f_4, and f_5 with p_2; and f_6 and f_7 with p_3. Clearly, we no longer wish to distinguish pairs of faults that are in the same package. Hence the contribution to a test weight due to such pairs should be subtracted from the weight. More formally, for test T_j, if

$$(n_0{}^j)_{b_k \cap p_l}$$

and

$$(n_1{}^j)_{b_k \cap p_l}$$

are, respectively, the numbers of zeroes and ones of the jth column which are in block b_k and are associated with package p_l, then

$$W_j{}^i = \sum_{k=1}^{m} \left[(n_0{}^j)_{b_k} \cdot (n_1{}^j)_{b_k} - \sum_{l} (n_0{}^j)_{b_k \cap p_l} \cdot (n_1{}^j)_{b_k \cap p_l} \right] \qquad (3.2)$$

where the summation $\sum_{l}$ is over all packages associated with block b_k.

Table 3.5a Fault Table

		t_1	t_2	t_3	t_4	t_5	t_6	t_7	t_8	
P_1	f_1^1	1	0	0	1	0	0	0	0	
	f_2^1	0	0	0	1	0	0	1	1	
P_2	f_1^2	0	0	1	1	0	1	0	0	
	f_2^2	0	1	0	1	0	0	1	1	
	f_3^2	0	1	0	0	0	0	1	0	
P_3	f_1^3	0	0	0	1	1	0	1	0 ←	
	f_2^3	1	1	0	0	0	1	0	1	Identical
P_4	f_1^4	0	0	0	1	1	0	1	0 ←	
	f_2^4	0	1	0	1	1	0	0	0	
	f_3^4	0	1	0	0	1	0	0	1	
P_5	f_1^5	1	0	1	0	1	1	0	0	
	f_2^5	0	1	1	0	1	1	0	0	
Weight =		24	30	25	30	35	29	29	26	

Here, an example from Chang (1965) will be helpful. Referring to Table 3.5a, we have a fault table of eight tests and twelve faults; the subject is realized with five circuit packages. To select an efficient set of tests, we first compute the initial weight W_j for each test. (The weights are recorded under the appropriate columns of the table.) We select the test of greatest weight, namely T_5. Next, we rearrange the fault table to form Table 3.5b, and the weights of all tests save T_5 are recomputed. This time T_6 gets the nod. To illustrate the weight computations, we give the details for W_6^1. Using equation 3.2,

$$
\begin{aligned}
W_6^1 &= \left[(n_0^6)_{b_1} \cdot (n_1^6)_{b_1} - \sum_l (n_0^6)_{b_1 \cap p_l} \cdot (n_1^6)_{b_1 \cap p_l} \right] \\
&\quad + \left[(n_0^6)_{b_2} \cdot (n_1^6)_{b_2} - \sum_l (n_0^6)_{b_2 \cap p_l} \cdot (n_1^6)_{b_2 \cap p_l} \right] \\
&= \{ (4 \cdot 2)_{b_1} - [(2 \cdot 0)_{b_1 \cap p_1} + (2 \cdot 1)_{b_1 \cap p_2} + (0 \cdot 1)_{b_1 \cap p_3} \\
&\quad + (0 \cdot 0)_{b_1 \cap p_4} + (0 \cdot 0)_{b_1 \cap p_5}] \} \\
&\quad + \{ (4 \cdot 2)_{b_2} - [(0 \cdot 0)_{b_2 \cap p_1} + (0 \cdot 0)_{b_2 \cap p_2} + (1 \cdot 0)_{b_2 \cap p_3} \\
&\quad + (3 \cdot 0)_{b_2 \cap p_4} + (0 \cdot 2)_{b_2 \cap p_5}] \} \\
&= 6 + 8 \\
&= 14.
\end{aligned}
$$

Table 3.5b First Rearrangement of Fault Table

		t_5	t_1	t_2	t_3	t_4	t_6	t_7	t_8	
P_1	f_1^1	0	1	0	0	1	0	0	0	
	f_2^1	0	0	0	0	1	0	1	1	
P_2	f_1^2	0	0	0	1	1	1	0	0	b_1
	f_2^2	0	0	1	0	1	0	1	1	
	f_3^2	0	0	1	0	0	0	1	0	
P_3	f_2^3	0	1	1	0	0	1	0	1	
P_3	f_1^3	1	0	0	0	1	0	1	0	
P_4	f_1^4	1	0	0	0	1	0	1	0	
	f_2^4	1	0	1	0	1	0	0	0	b_2
	f_3^4	1	0	1	0	0	0	0	1	
P_5	f_1^5	1	1	0	1	0	1	0	0	
	f_2^5	1	0	1	1	0	1	0	0	
Weight =		11	13	11	13	[14]	12	9		

The other weights are computed in exactly similar fashion. The next rearrangement of the fault table yields Table 3.5c. Notice here that block b_4 does not play any part in selecting the third test, since all rows (faults) of b_4 are associated with the same package (p_5). Thus there is no gain in considering b_4 any further.

Table 3.5c tell us to choose T_2 as the third test. After this is done, the next rearrangement yields Table 3.5d. Here, all tests have weights of zero, so the process terminates. The set $\{T_5, T_6, T_2\}$ is a minimal set having no redundancy. The result also shows that the number of entries in the fault table could be reduced. Instead of the original twelve fault patterns, only seven patterns are required to identify each faulty package. They are: $\mathbf{p}_1 = (0, 0, 0)$; $\mathbf{p}_2 = (0, 0, 1), (0, 1, 0)$; $\mathbf{p}_3 = (0, 1, 1), (1, 0, 0)$; $\mathbf{p}_4 = (1, 0, 0), (1, 0, 1)$; and $\mathbf{p}_5 = (1, 1, 0)$.

To conclude, this process appears to be an attractive one for handling large fault tables—the amount of storage required to perform it on a computer is relatively modest. It is also guaranteed to terminate, in no more than $\min(m, n)$ iterations. Indistinguishable faults are automatically grouped together, and test selection can be biased to accommodate any kind of circuit packaging constraints. The method is not guaranteed to produce a minimal set of tests; however, it frequently produces a near-minimal set.

Table 3.5c   Second Rearrangement of Fault Table

		t_5	t_6	t_1	t_2	t_3	t_4	t_7	t_8		
p_1	$f_1{}^1$	0	0	1	0	0	1	0	0		
	$f_2{}^1$	0	0	0	0	0	1	1	1	b_1	
p_2	$f_2{}^2$	0	0	0	1	0	1	1	1		
	$f_3{}^2$	0	0	0	1	0	0	1	0		
p_2	$f_1{}^2$	0	1	0	0	1	1	0	0	b_2	
p_3	$f_2{}^3$	0	1	1	1	0	0	0	1		
p_3	$f_1{}^3$	1	0	0	0	0	1	1	0		
	$f_1{}^4$	1	0	0	0	0	1	1	0		
p_4	$f_2{}^4$	1	0	0	1	0	1	0	0	b_3	
	$f_3{}^4$	1	0	0	1	0	0	0	1		
p_5	$f_1{}^5$	1	1	1	0	1	0	0	0	b_4	X
	$f_2{}^5$	1	1	0	1	1	0	0	0		X
	Weight =	3		$\boxed{7}$	1	3	5	4			

3.3.2   *Methods for Selecting Efficient Sequential Procedures.* One factor that strongly affects the efficiency of a sequential procedure is the method used to select the tests, just as was the case for combinational procedures. Now, however, there is an additional factor—the ordering of the tests in the procedure. Many of the methods for deriving efficient sequential procedures make use of some sort of figure of merit for tests. At each branch point in the procedure, several candidate tests (supplied either by an engineer or by one of the methods of Sections 3.1–3.2) are tried and evaluated. The one that maximizes the figure of merit is chosen. Procedures generated by this general approach are clearly not globally optimal—only local optimization has been done. However, many workers[26] have stated that such procedures are often close to the true minimum in cases where the true minimum is known. Conceptually, we can always find the true minimum by exhaustively trying all possibilities. However, in practice, this suggestion is even more ludicrous for sequential procedures than for combinational procedures. Not only would all possible sets of tests have to be tried but we also would have to take all possible permutations of all such sets.

In this subsection, we first discuss ways of constructing efficient sequential

---

[26] See, for example, Johnson (1960) or Kletsky (1960).

Table 3.5d   Third Rearrangement of Fault Table

		t_5	t_6	t_2	t_1	t_3	t_4	t_7	t_8	
p_1	f_1^1	0	0	0	1	0	1	0	0	b_1
	f_2^1	0	0	0	0	0	1	1	1	
p_2	f_2^2	0	0	1	0	0	1	1	1	b_2
	f_3^2	0	0	1	0	0	0	1	0	
p_2	f_1^2	0	1	0	0	1	1	0	0	b_3
p_3	f_1^3	0	1	1	1	0	0	0	1	b_4
$\rightarrow p_3$	f_1^3	1	0	0	0	0	1	1	0	h_5
$\rightarrow p_4$	f_1^4	1	0	0	0	0	1	1	0	
p_4	f_2^4	1	0	1	0	0	1	0	0	b_6
	f_3^4	1	0	1	0	0	0	0	1	
p_5	f_1^5	1	1	0	1	1	0	0	0 X	b_7
	f_2^5	1	1	1	0	1	0	0	0 X	
	Weight $=$				0	0	0	0	0	

procedures for fault detection. Next we discuss figures of merit which are useful in constructing sequential procedures for diagnosis.

In discussing minimal or near-minimal sequential procedures, we first must define what "minimal" means here. We shall call a sequential procedure for fault detection *minimal* if the branch of the diagnostic tree containing the fault-free machine has a minimal number of edges. We tacitly assume that the procedure is complete.

One figure of merit aimed at producing minimal procedures in this sense has been suggested by Seshu and Freeman (1962). They proposed that we select the test at each step of the procedure which detects the greatest number of hitherto-undetected faults. More formally, suppose that the equivalence classes of a diagnostic tree are coordinatized by the convention of Subsection 2.3.2 and that the failure-free machine is always carried in the top branch of the tree. Then Seshu's figure of merit for any test candidate T_j at the ith level of the procedure is

$$\alpha_j^i = \left. \frac{n(i, 1) - n(i + 1, 1)}{n(i, 1)} \right|_{T_j}$$

Here, $n(s, t)$ is the number of machines in equivalence class (s, t). The numerator thus computes the number of hitherto-undetected faults which T_j detects; the denominator serves to normalize this quantity.

As an example, consider the simulation data of Table 3.6a. To construct

Table 3.6a   Fault Table

	T_1	T_2	T_3	T_4	
M_1	z_1	z_2	z_2	z_4	(Good machine)
M_2	z_1	z_2	z_1	z_4	(Failure)
M_3	z_1	z_2	z_3	z_3	(Failure)
M_4	z_2	z_3	z_2	z_2	(Failure)
M_5	z_3	z_3	z_2	z_4	(Failure)
M_6	z_3	z_3	z_2	z_4	(Failure)
M_7	z_4	z_2	z_3	z_4	(Failure)
$\alpha_j{}^1$	$\boxed{.59}$	.43	.43	.28	

an efficient detection procedure, we compute the figure of merit for each test and list it under the appropriate column. T_1 is chosen as the first test, since it maximizes the figure of merit:

$$\alpha_1{}^0 = \left. \frac{n(0, 1) - n(1, 1)}{n(0, 1)} \right|_{T_1} = \frac{7 - 3}{7} = .59,$$

(as $n(0, 1) = n(0, j) = n(0, 0)$, for all j). If we eliminate the machines detected by T_1, the simulation data are as shown in Table 3.6b. The figures of

Table 3.6b   Reduced Fault Table

	T_1	T_2	T_3	T_4
M_1	z_1	z_2	z_2	z_4
M_2	z_1	z_2	z_1	z_4
M_3	z_1	z_2	z_3	z_3
$\alpha_j{}^2$	0	0	$\boxed{.66}$	.33

merit are recomputed, and T_3 is chosen. At this point the procedure is complete, and no more tests are needed. The test diagram for the procedure is given in Figure 3.33.

We now consider the construction of efficient sequential procedures for diagnosis. Many people have studied this problem; for example, Brulé et al. (1960), Chang (1968), and Kautz (1967). The two figures of merit that we shall describe are the *information gain* and the *distinguishability criterion*. Both methods fail to guarantee minimal procedures, but usually produce

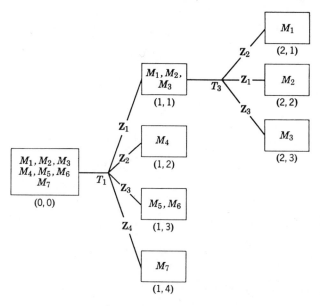

Figure 3.33   Test diagram.

efficient procedures. Again, we must state our definition of a minimal procedure. A sequential procedure for diagnosis is minimal if the average number of edges per branch of the test diagram is minimal. This average is weighted by the relative probabilities of occurrence of the failures associated with each branch.

The use of information gain as a figure of merit for testing was first proposed by Brulé et al. (1960). Following Shannon (1948), if p_j is the *a priori* probability that fault f_j will in fact occur, the uncertainty at the initial level of a test diagram is

$$A_0 = -\sum_j p_j \log_2 p_j. \tag{3.3}$$

Now the application of a test serves to remove some of this ambiguity; that is, it reduces our uncertainty as to the identity of the fault which is present in the subject. If we have a testing procedure of maximal diagnostic resolution (one machine per block of the final partition), the ambiguity associated with the final partition is clearly zero—the fault is always identified. Hence, the total amount of ambiguity removed (or, equivalently, information gained) along any branch of the diagram is equal to A_0, the ambiguity of the first level.

All of this suggests that the "best" next test at any step may be the one which results in the highest average information gain. For a test diagram in

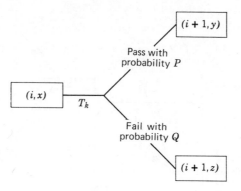

Figure 3.34   Branch point of a binary test diagram.

which all outcomes are binary (i.e., tests are passed or failed), the measure is

$$\overline{\Delta A_k} = A_{i,x} - (PA_{i+1,y} + QA_{i+1,z}) \tag{3.4}$$

Here

$\overline{\Delta A_k} \triangleq$ The average information gain due to test T_k at level i.

$A_{i,x} \triangleq$ The amount of ambiguity associated with equivalence class x, at level i.

$P \triangleq$ Probability that the test T_k will be passed.

$Q \triangleq 1 - P$.

Consequently, the quantity in parentheses is the amount of ambiguity associated with level $i + 1$. (All of this corresponds to the setup shown in Figure 3.34.) Moreover, faults in $(i + 1, y)$ and $(i + 1, z)$ are disjoint. Hence

$$P = \sum_{jy} p_{jx}, \qquad Q = \sum_{jz} p_{jx}$$

where p_{jx} is the probability that the jth fault will occur, evaluated at branch point (i, x) of the procedure. (Here, $\sum_{jy}$ denotes a sum over all members of (i, x) which T_k sends into $(i + 1, y)$.) Consequently, we can rewrite equation 3.4 as follows.

$$
\begin{aligned}
\overline{\Delta A_k} &= A_{i,x} - (PA_{i+1,y} + QA_{i+1,z}) \\
&= -\sum_{jx} p_{jx} \log_2 p_{jx} \\
&\quad - \left\{ \left(-\sum_{jy} p_{jy} \log_2 p_{jy} \right) + \left(-\sum_{jz} p_{jz} \log_2 p_{jz} \right) \right\} \\
&= -P \log_2 P - Q \log_2 Q \\
&= -P \log_2 P - (1 - P) \log_2 (1 - P) \tag{3.5}
\end{aligned}
$$

We can easily extend equation 3.5 to the case of nonbinary test outcomes. Here we observe output vectors during testing, rather than simply record "pass-or-fail"; let us suppose that (i, x) is partitioned into w equivalence classes as shown in Figure 3.35. Now the average information gain due to T_k becomes

$$\overline{\Delta A_k} = -\sum_{s=1}^{w} \left\{ \left[\sum_{jy_s} p_{jx} \right] \log_2 \left[\sum_{jy_s} p_{jx} \right] \right\} \tag{3.6}$$

If all faults are assumed to be equally probable, then the term $\sum_{jy_s} p_{jx}$ can be replaced by

$$\frac{n(i + 1, y_s)}{n(i, x)}.$$

Equation 3.6 then becomes

$$\overline{\Delta A_k} = -\sum_{s=1}^{w} \left\{ \frac{n(i + 1, y_s)}{n(i, x)} \log_2 \left[\frac{n(i + 1, y_s)}{n(i, x)} \right] \right\} \tag{3.7}$$

This figure of merit has also been suggested by Mandelbaum (1964). Moreover, it has been implemented in the Sequential Analyzer system of programs, as a criterion for test selection (see Chapter IV).

Finally, if C_k denotes the cost of test T_k, the criterion may be redefined to be

$$E_k = \frac{\overline{\Delta A_k}}{C_k}. \tag{3.8}$$

The *distinguishability criterion* for test selection is due to Chang (1968), and is similar to his technique for constructing combinational procedures. The basic idea is as follows.

At each branch point (i, x) in the test diagram, one would like to select a

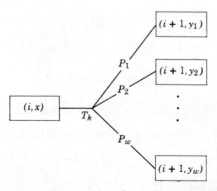

Figure 3.35 Branch point of a nonbinary test diagram.

test which distinguishes each machine in equivalence class (i, x) from every other machine in (i, x). There are a total of

$$\binom{n(i, x)}{2}$$

pairs of machines to be distinguished, and the test that comes closest to distinguishing all of these pairs should be selected.

Referring to Figure 3.35, if test T_k partitions class (i, x) into w equivalence classes, then T_k distinguishes every machine in $(i + 1, y_s)$ from every machine in $(i + 1, y_t)$, for $s \neq t$. The total number of pairs of machines distinguished by T_k is, therefore,

$$
\begin{aligned}
\gamma_k &= n(i + 1, y_1)[n(i + 1, y_2) + \cdots + n(i + 1, y_w)] \\
&\quad + n(i + 1, y_2)[n(i + 1, y_3) + \cdots + n(i + 1, y_w)] \\
&\quad + \cdots + n(i + 1, y_{w-1})[n(i + 1, y_w)] \\
&= \sum_{s=1}^{w-1} \left[n(i + 1, y_s) \sum_{t=s+1}^{w} n(i + 1, y_t) \right]
\end{aligned}
\tag{3.9}
$$

The value of γ_k attains its maximum of

$$\binom{n(i, x)}{2},$$

when $w = n(i, x)$; meaning that T_k uniquely identifies each of the $n(i, x)$ machines. It attains its minimum of zero when $w = 1$, meaning that no partitioning of class (i, x) occurred whatsoever.

The figure of merit γ_k can be generalized to allow for diagnosis to the level of replaceable packages, rather than individual components. The reasoning is identical to that followed in Chang's measure for combinational procedures; we simply deduct the contribution due to all fault pairs on the same packages from γ_k. Thus, if

$$n(i + 1, y_s)_p$$

is the number of machines in $(i + 1, y_s)$ which are associated with circuit package p, then

$$n(i + 1, y_s) = \sum_p n(i + 1, y_s)_p, \tag{3.10}$$

where $\sum_p$ is the sum over all packages associated with the failed machines of class $(i + 1, y_s)$. The number of machine pairs that should *not* be distinguished, therefore, is

$$\delta_k = \sum_{s=1}^{w-1} \left\{ \sum_p \left[n(i + 1, y_s)_p \cdot \sum_{t=s+1}^{w} n(i + 1, y_t)_p \right] \right\}. \tag{3.11}$$

Hence the generalized measure is

$$\lambda_k = \gamma_k - \delta_k$$

$$= \sum_{s=1}^{w-1} \left\{ \sum_p \left[n(i + 1, y_s)_p \cdot \sum_{t=s+1}^{w} \left(n(i + 1, y_t) - n(i + 1, y_t)_p \right) \right] \right\}. \quad (3.12)$$

An example of the use of this figure of merit to construct a sequential testing procedure can be found in Chang (1968).

3.3.3   Some Concluding Remarks.
We have described two kinds of techniques for selecting efficient test sets and sequences. The first kind is guaranteed to yield a minimal test sequence, but is prohibitively complicated for all but the smallest circuits of practical interest. Techniques of the second kind cannot be guaranteed to produce minimal procedures. However, they usually produce near-minimal results and, more important, they can be applied to practical situations.

This state of affairs may be unsatisfactory to the purist. However, we wish to point out that the practical difference between a minimal and near-minimal solution is usually insignificant. The economic consequences of a few extra words of mass storage or a few more milliseconds of testing time are trivial in most modern digital systems. The only valid reasons for pursuing minimal solutions are aesthetic or academic ones. We also suggest that the search for optimal solutions has been blown out of proportion in a good many other fields of engineering endeavor.

Experience suggests that most tests serve to detect a relatively small number of faults. The "ideal" test, which maximizes the value of a figure of merit, almost never seems to exist. In many cases,[27] a procedure designed for efficient fault detection also turns out to be efficient for fault diagnosis. However, there are pathological exceptions to this rule.

It appears, therefore, that a practical way to construct a good procedure for both detection and diagnosis is as follows. Initially, we select tests that provide efficient fault detection, using one or more of the appropriate figures of merit. After all faults have been detected, we assess the degree of diagnostic resolution that has resulted. If it is adequate (as it often is), we are done. If it is not, we then use figures of merit oriented toward diagnosis to select tests which further improve the diagnostic resolution. Alternatively, we can go back to the logic designers and ask for more access points to the circuitry under test.[28]

---

[27] See Subsection 4.4.2 for an example.
[28] The question of placement of access points has been discussed by Ramamoorthy (1967).

3.4   Methods of Fault Simulation

Fault simulation methods are used to predict the behavior of a digital system in the presence of a specified fault. They permit us to generate a mapping, called the *simulation data*, from fault identities to test outcomes. The simulation data, in turn, form the basis of the various *fault dictionaries* studied in Chapter V. The simulation data can also be used to determine the diagnostic resolution and completeness of the associated test set. This section is devoted to a comparative description of fault simulation methods. It is taken from Manning and Chang (1967).

Notice, first, that some of the formal procedures for test generation (such as the enf method and the *d*-algorithm) yield simulation data as a by-product. Thus the methods described here are of greatest value when the test set was *not* generated by such formal procedures.[29]

There are three widely used methods for simulating faults of digital systems: manual simulation, physical simulation and digital simulation. *Manual simulation* requires that an engineer analyze the system's behavior under failure "by hand"; that is, by manually tracing signals on logic diagrams. *Physical simulation* is the method of generating the simulation data by actually inserting failed components, one at a time, into a working model of the system, and then observing the results of running test programs. *Digital simulation* is the method of asking a computer program to predict the system's behavior under failure [Hardie and Suhocki (1966), Seshu and Freeman (1962)]. This section discusses these techniques and compares their merits and shortcomings.

Below is a list of assumptions shared by all three methods.

(a) The class of faults considered is finite and is known *a priori*.

(b) Failures are not intermittent.

(c) At most one fault has occurred since the last diagnosis—the so-called single-fault assumption.

In addition, the digital method requires us to assume that:

(d) Failures are logical. That is, insertion of any failure into the failure-free system (which, in general, is a sequential circuit) creates a new sequential circuit.

(e) The subject can be momentarily reset, even under failure, to a fixed, known, initial state.

---

[29] This is the case when the formal procedures fail; most notably, when the subject is a large digital system such as a processor. Here, an engineer familiar with the processor's design writes down a sequence of instructions whose execution hopefully exercises the hardware thoroughly. Fault simulation is then required to generate the simulation data and to check the engineer's work. Variants of this method of manual test generation are given in this section and in Section 4.4.

These assumptions should be familiar, since they have appeared at various places in Sections 3.1 and 3.2 in connection with test generation.

3.4.1 Manual Simulation. In its early years, the manual method was known as diagnostic programming. Its more recent manifestations are often called manual simulation. Diagnostic programs were oriented toward checking the instruction set of the system. Usually, each instruction was executed with random operands, followed by a simulation of the instruction using other instructions but the same operands. If the answers agreed, the instruction was assumed to be operative, and otherwise defective. Neither conclusion is necessarily valid. Consequently, such programs neither detected all hardware faults nor provided adequate diagnostic information.

More recently, the job of generating test programs and simulation data has been given to engineers familiar with the subject's logical design, and the simulation process has been renamed "manual simulation." The test programs are now oriented toward checking the hardware rather than the instruction repertoire of the machine. Consequently the simulation data (after processing to form some sort of fault dictionary) are often good enough to permit rapid repair. However, serious difficulties remain. We postpone discussion of these difficulties in order to give a brief description of the simulation process. Since the manual *simulation* technique historically has been closely linked with manual *test generation*, we describe both procedures.

A common approach to manual test generation for processors is the following. The engineer first conceptually partitions the subject into small, hardware-disjoint blocks. Each block should perform one, and preferably only one, logical function. Tests are then written (in terms of inputs and outputs of a block) that hopefully detect all faults of the block. (Here it is often possible to use the formal procedures of Sections 3.1 and 3.2. This would obviously improve the final results.) Next, the engineer tries to specify a sequence of subject machine instructions whose execution causes the tests to be applied. This job is repeated for each block of the subject, and the concatenated results form the diagnostic routine.[30]

Next, the engineer carries out manual fault simulation. For each test input and fault of a block, he must trace the output signals from the block outputs to the observable nodes of the subject (this often is a big job). Now the observable test outcomes for all faults are considered known, so the simulation is complete.

The manual method is very effective for small circuits. However, in handling digital systems having more than, say, 100 gates and 10 feedback lines, serious flaws appear. The first is *incompleteness*. The crucial single-fault assumption can only be validated if we have a test set that detects all faults,

---

[30] Another approach to manual test generation is described in Section 4.4.

and if we run the tests sufficiently often. Hence a primary purpose of any fault simulation method is to determine whether the test set is complete and, if not, to determine the undetected faults. The manual method will almost certainly yield an incomplete test set when it is applied to a large system, due to human error. Furthermore, there is no way to determine the undetected faults.

The second flaw is *inaccurate diagnostic data*. Here, again, the human is ill-suited to the job. Generating masses of simulation data by hand with no errors is a tough proposition, especially if the failed subject has races or oscillations. Finally, there is the problem of *test efficiency*. Recall that the test instruction sequence for each block is derived independently of the other blocks. But a given instruction sequence will, in fact, supply tests for many blocks in addition to the one intended by the designer. This inadvertent redundancy of tests tends to yield enormous diagnostic routines. Taken together, these three flaws should rule out use of the manual method for all but the smallest and simplest of subject circuits.

3.4.2 Physical Fault Simulation.

3.4.2 Physical Fault Simulation.   The physical simulation method was first described by Tsiang and Ulrich (1962). Their paper discussed the method, as used by Bell Telephone Laboratories, to treat machines used for electronic telephone switching. The BTL approach is actually a combined manual and physical one: the *tests* are generated manually, but the *simulation data* are generated by actually inserting faults into a model of the system and observing its behavior. Hence the completeness of the test set can be accurately determined, and the simulation data are relatively trustworthy. Thus the most serious flaws of manual simulation are overcome. Here we describe the method as used to treat the No. 1 Electronic Switching System (ESS).[31] However, the method is quite general and can be applied to other discrete-component machines.

The physical simulation setup for the No. 1 ESS is as follows. The system has a read-only store, which contains the diagnostic program and a simulation control program; and a writeable store which contains circuit package identities. (All of this is illustrated in Figure 3.36.) The system also has a scanner and central pulse distributor, which correspond to the I/O equipment of a general-purpose computer. In addition, a card reader, magnetic tape drive, Fault Simulation Unit (FSU) and Dictionary Control Unit (DCU) are supplied just for the fault simulation job. The cascade connection of the FSU and a modified circuit package[32] can simulate the good package or any

---

[31] Downing, Nowak, and Tuomenoksa (1964) have described the No. 1 ESS and its maintenance procedures.

[32] By *circuit package*, we mean the smallest replaceable module of a subject. These consist of ten or fewer gates, in the case of the No. 1 ESS central processor.

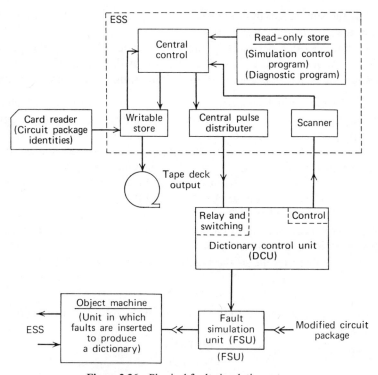

Figure 3.36   Physical fault simulation setup.

of the singly failed packages.[33] The selection of faults is controlled by the simulation control program via the DCU.

The simulation process begins with the loading of circuit package information into the writeable store. Then the FSU is interposed between a package and its socket, and the ESS central control starts to execute the control program. This causes signals to go to the DCU (via the central pulse distributor), which in turn sets up the first fault in the FSU. The ESS then executes the diagnostic tests, and the test results are written on tape. This process is repeated under program control until all faults of the package have been inserted. At this point, human intervention is required to move the FSU, change some connectors, replace the circuit package with another one, and restart the central control. When all faults of the entire ESS have been

---

[33] This is feasible only if a package is functionally simple. Also, the subject must be able to tolerate the extra line delays and noise introduced by the FSU. Hence the physical method would be inappropriate for subjects using Large Scale Integration technology or close timing tolerances.

inserted, the simulation data are processed by a general-purpose computer to generate the various fault dictionaries.

You should notice particularly that we execute all tests in the presence of the first fault, then all tests in the presence of the second fault, etc. The opposite time ordering occurs in digital simulation, which we describe next.

3.4.3   Digital Fault Simulation.   Digital fault simulation is the technique of predicting the behavior of a processor under failure by a computer program. The computer used to execute the program (the *host*) is generally different from the system being simulated (the subject). We now describe the digital simulation process from the user's viewpoint. Our description is somewhat brief, since a complete discussion of digital fault simulation is provided in Chapter IV. The simulator we describe in both instances is the Sequential Analyzer of S. Seshu (1962, 1965).

For concreteness, we shall assume that failures of the No. 1 ESS central control are to be treated. A coded description of the central control is assumed available as a file of the host's secondary storage. The directive

LØGIC,ESS1CC

tells the Analyzer to read in the description of the central control. Similarly, the directives

ØPTIØN
NØSHØRT

tell the Analyzer to omit shorted-diode faults. (Open diodes and output s–a–1 and s–a–0 faults are always treated.)

After some preliminary processing, the Analyzer puts out a list of all possible single faults of the specified types which the central control possesses. Next, it compiles the description of the central control into a subroutine called the *compiled simulator*. This routine can simulate the failure-free central control and all of the singly failed central controls.

Now two choices are available. If a manually generated test sequence is at hand, the user can say

MANUAL

followed by the test input vectors. The MANUAL directive causes the executive control program to talk directly to the manual test generation routine. The test input vectors are thus simply applied in sequence to the compiled simulator, which generates the system output vectors corresponding to each fault. After suitable processing these are put out as the simulation data. (Notice that the first test input vector is simulated for all faults, then the second vector is simulated for all faults, etc., in exact contradistinction to the time ordering followed in physical simulation.)

Alternately, the user may have no manually-generated tests. In this case he can say

AUTØMATIC

causing the Analyzer to attempt automatic test generation. Here, then, the Analyzer's output is both the tests *and* the simulation data. The AUTØMATIC directive causes the executive control program to activate the automatic test generation routine, which in turn calls on a set of heuristic subroutines[34] to generate the tests. (As in the MANUAL mode, the test input vectors are applied to the compiled simulator to create the diagnostic data.) Now the AUTØMATIC mode may fail to produce an adequate test sequence, since the test generation subroutines are heuristic rather than algorithmic. However, the user can freely switch between the two modes, in order to append manually-generated tests to an automatically generated sequence. These processes of man-machine cooperation and automatic test generation have only limited counterparts in the world of physical fault simulation.

3.4.4 Comparisons. In this subsection we compare the virtues of the physical and digital methods as tools for producing simulation data, for aiding hardware and diagnostic program design, and for research in fault diagnosis. The manual method is not considered because of the grave defects that it possesses.

Both the physical method and the digital method are reasonable choices for production of fault dictionaries. Both methods generate the simulation data automatically, so that human errors will be relatively infrequent. Also, the exact subset of faults which are undetected is known. Thus both techniques overcome the main defects of the manual method.

At present, the physical method probably retains its edge over the digital method in machine time required to generate simulation data.[35] The physical method can treat a wider class of faults, and can be applied to "nonlogical" units such as I/O equipment. However, the method is very inflexible. It requires that the subject system, the special hardware, and the simulation control program be in perfect condition.[36] Also, the diagnostic hardware

[34] The subroutines implement the heuristics described in Subsection 3.2.2.

[35] We have derived an upper bound of 1600 hours of IBM 360/65 time to produce simulation data for the central control of the No. 1 ESS. In addition, the use of functional simulation techniques (see Section 6.1) is expected to reduce simulation time by a factor of 2 or 3. On the other hand, the physical method requires 1000 hours of No. 1 ESS time for the same job.

[36] The digital method makes the analogous demand, that the host machine and the coded description of the subject be in perfect condition. Thus both methods require that one digital system (the subject or the host) be guaranteed free of failures before the diagnosis procedures can be simulated. This paradox has led to a good deal of philosophical speculation which is irrelevant here.

and software cannot be evaluated until fault simulation and dictionary production are complete. It is usually impossible to make major design changes
at this late date in the development schedules. Finally, the method is vulner-
able to human error, because of the frequent human intervention required
during simulation.

The digital method is less general. However, since less human intervention
is required, there is less inaccuracy due to human error. In the case where
many versions of a system are to be built, the digital method is helpful, for
we need only provide a few reels of tape containing the coded description of
each version. Under physical simulation, one must either reconfigure the
laboratory model or provide many laboratory models. Finally, the impact
of integrated circuitry looms over the future of any simulation method. The
feasibility of performing physical insertion of faults on a system built with
Large Scale Integration technology is questionable. Here, then, the digital
method has the edge. Simulation of the class of faults that we have assumed
is as easy for integrated circuits as for discrete ones.

We now consider the methods as aids in hardware system and diagnostic
program design. Here, physical simulation is of very limited value. The cost
of constructing prototypes of many systems for studies in "diagnosable
design" is prohibitive. On the other hand, the digital method shows considerable promise. One can derive diagnostic procedures to determine the
fraction of undetectable faults, the adequacy of diagnostic hardware, the
general suitability of the design, and so on. If the design is unsatisfactory, it
can be redone before any specifications are frozen. We cannot insist too
strongly on the need for this approach to processor design.[37]

Just as a premature commitment to hardware can be avoided by digital
fault simulation, so can premature commitment to diagnostic programs be
prevented. To illustrate this point, note that program designers using physical
simulation cannot check their work until: the entire program has been written;
the physical simulation job has been completed; and the simulation data
have been processed to create a fault dictionary.

---

[37] We have been trying the good will of our friends in logic design with the following
observation. To design a hardware system with no thought to diagnosability, and to then
hand the frozen design to the fault diagnosis people, can only have one outcome. The
diagnostician can state the causes of the design's death, but he cannot bring it back to life!
(The identical situation has been faced by statisticians working in the life sciences, where
some scientists are fond of designing and performing experiments; and only then calling in
the statistician to make sense of the results.) Thus, there is a real need for logic designers to
become more familiar with diagnosis problems, and to work closely with the diagnosticians
during the design of a system. The use of a fault simulator during the design cycle, as suggested above, is one good way to cope with these new constraints on logic design. The
formulation of design principles for "diagnosability" (see Section 4.4) is another. However,
we are far from having a really complete, adequate set of principles. The help of logic
design specialists is urgently needed to advance our understanding of this whole area.

The use of a digital simulator can solve this problem. Here, production of the dictionary can proceed *concurrently* with the design of the tests; indeed, a new "partial dictionary" can be generated as each new block of tests is added to the test sequence. Hence the test designer can know the exact impact of all previous tests before he writes the next block. Therefore, mistakes and inefficiencies in test design and encoding are immediately apparent and can be easily corrected.

This vital difference between the two methods is a direct consequence of the difference in time ordering of simulation. One cannot produce a sequence of "partial dictionaries" under physical simulation because one must simulate *all* tests with the first fault, followed by all tests with the second fault, etc. Hence the test designer who relies exclusively on the physical method must give up an important source of immediate feedback.

Finally, we come to research in fault diagnosis. The physical method is of limited use here, since each new idea may require the detailed design and construction of a prototype system embodying that idea. As the digital method requires only the coded description of the logic[38] of a new machine, research is facilitated.

3.4.5 Summary and Conclusions. The method of manual simulation has grave defects that should exclude it from consideration. This is especially true if the subject is large or complex. We have argued that both the physical and digital methods of fault simulation have unique, valuable advantages. The physical method seems well suited to final production of simulation data for discrete-component processors, and to treating faults of "nonlogical" equipment such as peripheral devices. The digital method shines in research and development applications, and in dealing with integrated circuitry. Consequently, both methods should be used in the development of a digital system. Only in this way can the best possible diagnostics be obtained.

The digital simulation method is the most flexible and interesting of the three. Yet we have described it briefly, and from the user's point of view. We now consider, more thoroughly, a modern simulator: the Sequential Analyzer.

---

[38] It may not even be necessary to specify the logic on the gate level of fine detail. See Section 6.1.

CHAPTER IV

The Sequential Analyzer

We have seen that digital fault simulation is well suited to several problems in automated fault diagnosis. Therefore, it is important to examine the techniques of digital fault simulation in some detail. We shall do this by studying a particular modern simulator—the Sequential Analyzer—which was designed and described by the late Professor S. Seshu (1962, 1964, 1965).

The Sequential Analyzer is a set of computer programs that can generate fault simulation data for a given logic circuit, class of faults, and test sequence. It also has the unique ability of generating tests automatically for combinational and sequential circuits. In this chapter, we first outline the Analyzer's capabilities briefly, from the user's point of view (Section 4.1). (Part of the material has been presented previously, but it is collected here for completeness and easy reference.) Next, we shift somewhat toward the programmer's point of view by outlining some of the internal flow of control and data during a small problem run (Section 4.2). The shift of viewpoint becomes pronounced in Section 4.3, where we describe the structure of certain key programs in detail. Finally, we turn from the Analyzer itself to an account of its applications in automated fault diagnosis. This material, together with a critical look at the merits and shortcomings of the present version of the system, comprises the final section of the chapter. The reader might take advantage of this organization by skipping Sections 4.2 and 4.3 on a first reading.

4.1 What It Does

The Analyzer is a digital fault simulator. That is, one can give it a coded description of a digital circuit, a specification of permissible failure modes, and a sequence of tests as input data. From these, the Analyzer will produce the associated simulation data. This capability is typical of digital fault simulators. In addition, the Analyzer has the unique ability of generating tests automatically. We now review the major features of the system very briefly.

As we noted in Section 3.4, the directive

LØGIC,NAME

is used to retrieve and read in the coded description of the subject circuit NAME. The directive

ØPTIØN

is used to supply the specification of permissible failure modes, as well as many other options. There are two possible modes for test generation. The directive

MANUAL

tells the Analyzer that the user will supply a sequence of test input vectors. Alternately, the directive

AUTØMATIC

tells the Analyzer to attempt automatic test generation. The automatic test generation driver calls on four routines which implement the heuristics described in Subsection 3.2.2. Tests are evaluated by computing a figure of merit, and the first test found whose figure exceeds a threshold value is used. Currently, the user can choose between two figures of merit, selected by the ØPTIØN cards

CHECKØUT

and   INFØ.

The CHECKØUT figure of merit is defined as the number of faults distinguished from the good machine, divided by the total number of faults being simulated. It is useful when the user wishes to derive a test sequence for fault detection. The INFØ figure of merit computes the information gain of a test, taken over the probabilities of occurrence of the various failures. It is useful when the user wishes to derive a test sequence for fault diagnosis. These and related measures were discussed extensively in Subsection 3.3.2.

It is clear from this summary of features that the Sequential Analyzer is a remarkably powerful tool. However, it is naturally subject to a number of assumptions and limitations. The assumptions are as follows:

1. The class of faults considered is finite and is known *a priori*.
2. Faults are logical.
3. Faults are not intermittent.
4. It is possible to *momentarily* reset the subject's feedback lines, *even under failure*, to a fixed, known initial state.
5. At most one fault has occurred since the last diagnosis (the single-fault assumption).

The programs are currently implemented in assembly language for the Control Data 3600 computer, with one to four banks of core memory. Assuming the use of four banks of core memory, the following limitations apply.

1. Maximum of 3000 gates.
2. Maximum of 5000 faults.
3. Maximum of 96 primary inputs.
4. Maximum of 96 primary outputs.
5. Maximum of 48 feedback lines.
6. Asynchronous or ideal synchronous circuit operation.
7. No hazard analysis.

A few comments about these assumptions and limitations are in order. Assumption *2* states that insertion of any fault into a sequential circuit creates another sequential circuit. For discrete transistor-diode circuits, we allow open and shorted[1] input diodes, gate outputs s–a–0, and gate outputs s–a–1. Assumption *4* states that we can seize the feedback lines and force them into a specified state. However, when we release the lines, the subject may undergo transitions before entering a stable state. Moreover, it may undergo different transitions leading to different stable states for the various faults. (Hence the word *momentarily*.) Assumption *5* is justified by insisting on a complete test set and by diagnosing relatively often. Thus the probability of occurrence of two independent faults can be made acceptably small.

Turning to the limitations of the programs, the first two items are solely due to the quantity of core memory available. They can be traded off, one for the other, by simply changing two program parameters and reassembling. (This is not true of the other limitations. Here, both additional memory and reprogramming would be required.) Also, one can always divide the faults of a large subject into several sets, and treat each set in a separate simulation run.

The upper limit of 48 feedback loops applies to loops that are independent in the graph-theoretic sense. It need not include flip-flops, since these can be handled by a special method (the macro gate technique, described in Subsection 6.1.1). Finally, notice that asynchronous circuits are simulated in terms of the Huffman model. Race analysis is performed and oscillations are detected. Synchronous circuits are handled by a very simple model with no timing analysis. In neither case is hazard analysis done.

We have observed what the Analyzer can do. Now let us see how it does it. This is the topic of the next section.

---

[1] The modelling of shorted diodes is not particularly realistic in the present version of the system.

4.2 An Analyzer Run

Here we give a step-by-step description of a small, simple fault simulation. Our aim is to describe each step from the user's point of view, and simultaneously to sketch what is happening behind the scenes. Such a discussion must, of course, be incomplete and highly simplified. Consequently, we describe a few key programs in greater detail in Section 4.3. The reader who wishes to explore more deeply is referred to Professor Seshu's writings, particularly Seshu (1964).

Consider the simple, asynchronous circuit EXAMPLE, shown in Figure 4.1. The coded description of EXAMPLE is given in Figure 4.2. The INPUTS and ØUTPUTS statements specify primary inputs and outputs of the circuit, at which test input vectors can be applied and outputs observed. The FEEDBK statement specifies the gates whose outputs realize the feedback output functions $\{Y_i\}$ of the Huffman model (Section 2.1). This information is required both to establish the Huffman model of the given circuit and to organize the logic, as discussed below.

The remainder of the coded description consists of the gate declarations. Each gate is specified as to type and name, and the number and names of the gates and/or inputs which feed it are declared. (Additionally, the names of the gates which it feeds may be declared. If this is done, it is possible to check for coding errors by comparing the two descriptions of the circuit thus supplied.) Notice the asterisk after the $R1$ input to gate $A2$. This says that $A2$ is the first gate of a feedback loop whose last gate is $R1$. ($R1$ might well feed additional gates, which are not the first gates of feedback loops having $R1$ as last gate. For such gates the asterisk would be omitted.)

The run begins with a separate preprocessor, the LØGIC ØRGANIZER program. The purpose of this program is to impose a partial ordering on the gates, which makes the tasks of logic compilation and simulation easier and more efficient. After the gate declarations have been partially ordered, the ØRGANIZER circuit description is passed on to the Analyzer proper.

The LØGIC ØRGANIZER contains a control program READCNTR (Read and Control), which reads and obeys the user's command directives. (This

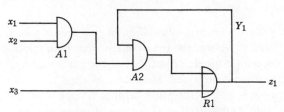

Figure 4.1 Logic circuit EXAMPLE.

	IDENT	EXAMPLE	
INPUTS	3		
	X1	X2	X3
OUTPUTS	1		
	R1		
FEEDBK	1		
	R1		
R1	ØR	2	
	A2	X3	
A1	AND	2	
	X1	X2	
A2	AND	2	
	A1	R1 *	

Figure 4.2   Coded description of EXAMPLE.

program permits the use of a natural, problem-oriented command language.) Assume that the coded description of Figure 4.2 exists as a file in some medium which has been designated as system input. The user's first command directive is

LØGIC,EXAMPLE

issued via the system control medium. (On the CDC 3600, both the input medium and the control medium are frequently magnetic tape drives.) READCNTR analyzes and obeys the directive, causing a search of the system input medium for a file whose name is EXAMPLE. When the file is found, it is read into the host computer's main storage, record by record. Extensive format and consistency checking are performed, permitting us to detect most of the common errors found in circuit descriptions. The circuit description is actually stored in main storage as a set of lists.

As we have said, the main purpose of the LØGIC ØRGANIZER is to impose a partial ordering on the gates of a circuit. The ordering is defined recursively as follows.

1. A gate G is of level 1 iff all of its inputs are primary or feedback inputs of the circuit;
2. A gate G is of level n iff all of its inputs are of level $n - 1$ or less, and at least one input is of level $n - 1$.

This partial ordering ensures that all gates that feed a gate G are of lower level than G. Thus, if we sort the list of gate names by level, a top-to-bottom scan will not encounter a gate G until all of the gates that feed G have been seen. This partial ordering is of great convenience to the logic compiler, which replaces each gate description with a fragment of code capable of simulating the gate. Our partial ordering therefore ensures that the compiled simulator will not attempt to compute any gate's output value until it has computed all of its input values. Finally, notice that this partial ordering is a close relative of the full ordering used in the *d*-algorithm (Subsection 3.1.3).

The organizing process is activated by the single user command

ØRGANIZE

The gates are assigned level numbers, the gate declarations are sorted by level number, and the sorted circuit description is written on the ØRGAN-IZER's output medium. The result of organizing the circuit EXAMPLE is shown in Figure 4.3.

Now, the algorithm used to partially order the gates requires that all feedback loops have been broken, by declaring feedback inputs and outputs. If the user fails to break some loop, the algorithm fails and the run will terminate with a message on the error message medium. The ØRGANIZER will also put out a list specifying a set of gates that contains the unbroken loop.[2]

In any event, EXAMPLE has been ØRGANIZEd successfully, so the user may begin to use the Analyzer proper. His first directive is

LØGIC,EXAMPLE

This is issued to a copy of READCNTR embedded in the Analyzer. This time, the ØRGANIZEd circuit description is read in and stored as a set of lists in

	IDENT	EXAMPLE		
INPUTS	3			
	X1	X2	X3	
OUTPUTS	1			
	R1			
FEEDBK	1			
	R1			
A1	AND	2		LEVEL 1
	X1	X2		
A2	AND	2		LEVEL 2
	A1	R1 *		
R1	ØR	2		LEVEL 3
	A2	X3		

Figure 4.3   ØRGANISEd description of EXAMPLE.

[2] The problem of locating feedback loops is not severe for the very simple circuit EXAMPLE. However, it is definitely severe for many of the complex circuits found in a digital processor. For these circuits, one expects to make many attempts to ØRGANISE the circuit description, locating a few more feedback loops at each attempt. An ØRGANISER run requires about one minute of CDC 3600 time for the largest circuits which the present Analyzer can handle. Also, extensive editing facilities are provided for declaring additional feedback loops "on line." Thus this is a practical approach in many cases. Alternatively, the work of Ramamoorthy (1967) provides an elegant, analytical procedure for locating feedback loops.

main memory. Now the user may supply some reset states for **EXAMPLE**. This is done by saying, for example,

RESETS,2

0 0

4 7

These are coded in octal with trailing zeros. The feedback reset states are given first, separated by single spaces from the primary input vectors. Thus the above directive supplies the resets

$$\mathbf{y} = (0); \qquad \mathbf{X} = (0, 0, 0);$$

and

$$\mathbf{y} = (1); \qquad \mathbf{X} = (1, 1, 1).$$

READCNTR stores these on a list of permissible resets. Control options are set up by the directive

ØPTIØN

followed by the options; for example

NØSHØRT,MØNITØR,.

This causes system flags to be set specifying "no compilation of shorted diodes," and "go to the next problem if any difficulties arise."

Now, the user has the choice of **MANUAL** or **AUTØMATIC** modes for test generation.[3] These respectively imply user-supplied tests or tests generated automatically by the Analyzer. Suppose that the user has some manually-generated tests. The next command directive, then, is obviously

MANUAL

The next step is to compile a simulation subroutine for **EXAMPLE**. This is done by issuing the directive

SUBSET,0,0

which initiates a chain of events partially illustrated in Figure 4.4. (The reason for the choice of name for this directive will be clear shortly.) First, a general initialization of Analyzer constants and list pointers is performed. A cursory attempt is then made to determine whether the core image of the Analyzer is intact and serviceable. If it is not, the message LOAD FRESH PROGRAM is put out on the error medium and the run is aborted. If the programs do seem serviceable, control passes to the logic compiler.

The compiler performs two major functions: (1) it scans the gate declarations of **EXAMPLE** (Figure 4.3), and (2) it puts out a simulation fragment of

---

[3] The directives SIMULATE and DIAGNØSE were used as synonyms for MANUAL and AUTØMATIC in early versions of the Sequential Analyzer.

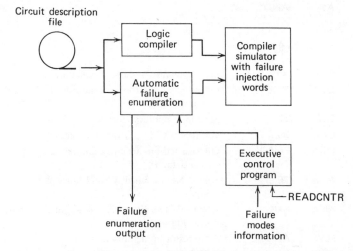

Figure 4.4 Program flow during logic compilation.

code for each gate.[4] The fragments are concatenated in the same order as the ØRGANIZEd gate declarations, for the reasons discussed above. Notice that the compiled simulator thus obtained can simulate as many failures *at once* as the host computer has bits in its words. This technique is called *parallel simulation*, and permits each pass through the simulator to treat 48 failures. (The CDC 3600 has 48-bit words.)

Failures are injected into the compiled simulator by using *failure injection words*. This technique is illustrated in Figure 4.5. The second major function of the logic compiler is therefore as follows. The compiler enumerates the failures of **EXAMPLE**, and a failure injection word is made up for each failure. (A failure injection word is always either all 1's or all 0's, with the possible exception of one bit which is complemented to inject a failure.)

Next, a routine to put out the enumeration of failures is entered. This produces the output shown in Figure 4.6.[5] Finally, control is returned to the executive control program **READCNTR**, to acquire the user's next command directive. We shall discuss the logic compiler in more detail in Section 4.3.

The user can now begin the fault-simulation process, by simulating the application of a reset to **EXAMPLE** and to the versions of **EXAMPLE** having single faults. (The latter are the so-called *failed machines*.) This step, the

---

[4] The correspondence between gate declarations and simulation fragments is very simple, and is illustrated in Figure 4.5. Although the Analyzer actually uses CDC 3600 assembly language, the simulation fragment is given in 7090 FAP. This is done in the hope that FAP is intelligible to the larger number of readers.

[5] Machine 1 is always the failure-free one, by convention.

	A1	AND	2
	X1	X2	

$$\Updownarrow$$

	CAL	X1	Get input $X1$ for current machines.
*	ORA	FAIL 1	OR selected bits to inject failures of $X1$ input (s–a–1 fault).
	SLW	TEMP	Save in temporary storage.
	CAL	X2	Get input $X2$ for current machines.
*	ORA	FAIL 2	OR selected bits to inject failures of $X2$ input (s–a–1 fault).
*	ANA	TEMP	Take AND of failed $X1$ and failed $X2$ inputs.
*	ANA	FAIL 3	AND selected bits to inject output (or input) s–a–0 fault.
*	SLW	A1	Store result in memory area for gate $A1$.

Figure 4.5   Correspondence between gate declarations and simulation fragments (in FAP).

necessary first step in simulation of a test sequence, is accomplished by the directive

RESET,1

This directive selects the first reset from the list of permissible resets, in this case, $y = (0)$, $X = (0, 0, 0)$, and applies it to all machines, both failure-free and singly failed. The output that results is given in Figure 4.7. To comprehend it, we must digress for a moment.

Recall that we may think of a test sequence as a multiple gedanken-experiment performed on many copies of a sequential machine, each one having a different single fault. Moreover, we may represent the experiment as a test diagram or tree. (These concepts were discussed at length in Section 2.3, and they form the conceptual basis of the Sequential Analyzer.) Thus, the Analyzer output resulting from the RESET,1 directive, as shown in Figure 4.7, is equivalent to the test diagram of Figure 4.8. (Machine 1 is always placed in the uppermost branch of the tree, by convention.) In this context, SUBSET,0,0 says to begin simulation at the root of the test tree, which implies program initialization and compilation of a simulator. Hence our choice of name for this directive.

The gross program flow that generates the output of Figure 4.7 can be explained with the help of Figure 4.9. When the user issues the RESET,1 directive, the mode switch has already been set to manual test generation (by the MANUAL directive), and the compiled simulator has been created

ENUMERATION OF MACHINE FAILURES FOR LOGIC CIRCUIT EXAMPLE

MACH NOS	FAILURE	MACH NOS	FAILURE	MACH NOS	FAILURE	MACH NOS	FAILURE
1	GOOD MACHINE	2	X1 TO A1 OPEN	3	X2 TO A1 OPEN	4	A1 OUTPUT 0
5	A1 OUTPUT 1	6	A1 TO A2 OPEN	7	R1 TO A2 OPEN	8	A2 OUTPUT 0
9	A2 OUTPUT 1	10	A2 TO R1 OPEN	11	X3 TO R1 OPEN	12	R1 OUTPUT 0
13	R1 OUTPUT 1						

INPUT ORDER X1 X2 X3
OUTPUT ORDER R1
FB ORDER R1

Figure 4.6 Enumeration of failures for EXAMPLE.

<pre>
                      FEEDBACK INPUT   0
                      PRIMARY INPUT   0 0 0
PRIMARY INPUT   0 0 0
INDEX OF OUTPUT SET   (1, 1)
OUTPUT VECTOR   0
MACHINE NUMBERS   1 2 3 4 5 6 7 8 10 11 12
INDEX OF OUTPUT SET   (1, 2)
OUTPUT VECTOR   1
MACHINE NUMBERS   9 13
</pre>

Figure 4.7   Initial output for fault simulation (level 1).

(by SUBSET,0,0). The RESET,1 directive causes the executive control program READCNTR to retrieve the proper initial values for the primary and feedback inputs of EXAMPLE. READCNTR passes these to the race analysis program, PROGRAM HUFFMAN, which, in turn, supplies them as input data to the compiled simulator. As failed machines are simulated in groups of 48, the bookkeeping routines cut up the set of failed machines appropriately, and set up the failure injection words for the first group of 48 machines in the compiled simulator. Control then passes to the compiled simulator, which computes the feedback output vector Y and the primary output vector Z for each of the current group of 48 machines. The simulator then returns control to its calling program, PROGRAM HUFFMAN. PROGRAM HUFFMAN compares the feedback input vector y with the feedback output vector Y, for each machine in the current group of 48. If $Y = y$ for a machine, the machine is in a stable state and requires no further processing. If y and Y differ in exactly one bit, one feedback line is unstable. In this case, y is set equal to Y and the compiled simulator is executed again. If y and Y differ in two or more bits for a machine, a race exists. In this case the compiled simulator is

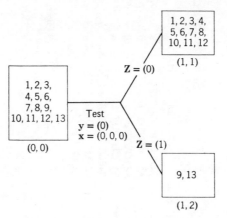

Figure 4.8   Test diagram or diagnostic tree for Figure 4.7 (level 1).

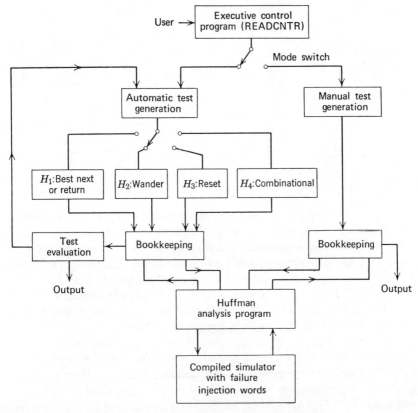

Figure 4.9   Program flow during fault simulation.

reconfigured to follow the various race branches for this machine. If the race branches all eventually lead to the same stable state, this state is recorded as the new value of **y** for the machine, and the race is declared noncritical. No messages are put out, and the user is unaware that a noncritical race has occurred. If further simulation shows that the various race branches lead to two or more different stable states, the race is declared critical. In this case, an appropriate message is put out on the error message medium, and the machine in question is discarded. (That is, it is not simulated for any subsequent test inputs.) If the number of race branches exceeds 48 at any point, the compiled simulator cannot follow the race any further. (Each bit of the 48-bit words is being used to follow one race branch.) Here, too, an error message is put out and the machine is discarded.

In summary, then, PROGRAM HUFFMAN serves to "close the feedback lines" of the simulated circuits, both failure-free and failed. The compiled

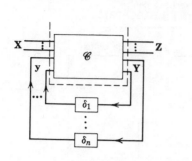 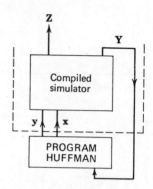

Figure 4.10 Correspondence between analyzer routines and the Huffman model.

simulator simulates the action of the combinational logic. This correspondence is shown in Figure 4.10. Let us also notice here the procedure used to simulate synchronous circuits. In this case, PROGRAM HUFFMAN simply sets $\mathbf{y} = \mathbf{Y}$ for all machines, thus making the present feedback output vector the new feedback input vector, for the next test input. This corresponds roughly to the action of the clock pulse in closing the feedback lines of a well-designed synchronous circuit. We shall supplement this brief discussion of PROGRAM HUFFMAN with a more detailed discussion in Section 4.3.

After the first group of 48 machines has been processed, we return from PROGRAM HUFFMAN to bookkeeping. The new feedback input and primary output vectors are recorded, and the failure injection words for the next group of 48 machines are set up in the simulator. Then control is passed to PROGRAM HUFFMAN again. This loop is repeated until all of the machines have been simulated.[6] Finally, complicated bookkeeping routines are entered which sort all of the machines by output vector, make up the new partition of machines, and print the results. Control is then passed back to READCNTR to acquire the user's next directive.

Now that the application of a reset has been simulated, the user can give his sequence of test input vectors. To do so, he says

SEQUENCE

followed by the test input vectors, one per card image, coded in octal as before. For example,

SEQUENCE
1

applies the vector

$$\mathbf{X} = (0, 0, 1)$$

[6] The loop is only executed once per test input for EXAMPLE, since EXAMPLE generates fewer than 48 machines.

INDEX OF INPUT SET	(1, 1)
PRIMARY INPUT	0 0 1
INDEX OF OUTPUT SET	(2, 1)
OUTPUT VECTOR	1
MACHINE NUMBERS	1 2 3 4 5 6 7 8 10
INDEX OF OUTPUT SET	(2, 2)
OUTPUT VECTOR	0
MACHINE NUMBERS	11 12

Figure 4.11   Further output for fault simulation (level 2).

to the machines of subset, or equivalence class, or diagnostic tree leaf (1, 1). (This creates the printout, or refined partition, or grown tree shown in Figures 4.11 and 4.12.) Only one tree branch can be followed at a time. The program will normally follow the uppermost branch. However, the directive

SUBSET,I,J

can be used to initiate simulation of a new tree branch. Here, (I, J) can be the coordinates of any leaf of the diagnostic tree at the time the SUBSET directive is given. The user can continue in this manner until he has simulated all of his test sequence on the uppermost branch. He can then use the SUBSET directive to carry the other branches of the test diagram through part or all of the test sequence, if he wishes. Thus the Analyzer allows considerable flexibility in the manner in which the diagnostic tree is "grown." Early

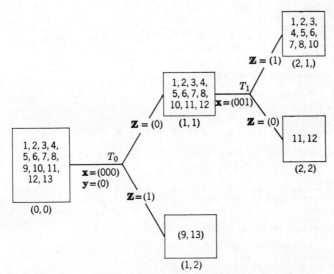

Figure 4.12   Grown diagnostic tree for Figure 4.11 (level 2).

termination, combinational testing (i.e., apply the same test sequence to all branches), or sequential testing (different sequences for different branches) can all be simulated with equal ease.

Let us suppose that the user has now exhausted his supply of manually generated tests. He can ask the automatic test generation facility to carry on, by issuing the directives

ENDMANUAL

AUTØMATIC

This resets the mode switch shown in Figure 4.9. Options for the AUTØMATIC

```
        FEEDBACK INPUT   0
          PRIMARY INPUT  000
PRIMARY INPUT            000
INDEX OF OUTPUT SET  (    1,    1)
OUTPUT VECTOR            0
MACHINE NUMBERS          1    2    3    4    5    6    7    8   10   11   12
INDEX OF OUTPUT SET  (    1,    2)
OUTPUT VECTOR            1
MACHINE NUMBERS          9   13


INDEX OF INPUT SET   (    1,    1)
PRIMARY INPUT            001
INDEX OF OUTPUT SET  (    2,    1)
OUTPUT VECTOR            1
MACHINE NUMBERS          1    2    3    4    5    6    7    8   10
INDEX OF OUTPUT SET  (    2,    2)
OUTPUT VECTOR            0
MACHINE NUMBERS         11   12


INDEX OF INPUT SET   (    2,    1)
PRIMARY INPUT            000
INDEX OF OUTPUT SET  (    3,    1)
OUTPUT VECTOR            0
MACHINE NUMBERS          1    2    3    4    7    8   10
INDEX OF OUTPUT SET  (    3,    2)
OUTPUT VECTOR            1
MACHINE NUMBERS          5    6
         CURRENT STRATEGY  WANDER

INDEX OF INPUT SET   (    3,    1)
PRIMARY INPUT            010
INDEX OF OUTPUT SET  (    4,    1)
OUTPUT VECTOR            0
MACHINE NUMBERS          1    2    3    4    7    8   10

INDEX OF INPUT SET   (    4,    1)
PRIMARY INPUT            110
INDEX OF OUTPUT SET  (    5,    1)
OUTPUT VECTOR            0
MACHINE NUMBERS          1    2    3    4    8   10
INDEX OF OUTPUT SET  (    5,    2)
OUTPUT VECTOR            1
MACHINE NUMBERS          7
         CURRENT STRATEGY  WANDER

INDEX OF INPUT SET   (    5,    1)
PRIMARY INPUT            100
INDEX OF OUTPUT SET  (    6,    1)
OUTPUT VECTOR            0
MACHINE NUMBERS          1    2    3    4    8   10
```

```
INDEX OF INPUT SET  (    6,    1)

PRIMARY INPUT           101
INDEX OF OUTPUT SET (    7,    1)
OUTPUT VECTOR           1
MACHINE NUMBERS         1    2    3    4    8    10

INDEX OF INPUT SET  (    7,    1)
PRIMARY INPUT           100
INDEX OF OUTPUT SET (    8,    1)
OUTPUT VECTOR           0
MACHINE NUMBERS         1    2    4    8    10
INDEX OF OUTPUT SET (    8,    2)
OUTPUT VECTOR           1
MACHINE NUMBERS         3
           CURRENT STRATEGY   WANDER

INDEX OF INPUT SET  (    8,    1)
PRIMARY INPUT           110
INDEX OF OUTPUT SET (    9,    1)
OUTPUT VECTOR           0
MACHINE NUMBERS         1    2    4    8    10


INDEX OF INPUT SET  (    9,    1)
PRIMARY INPUT           111
INDEX OF OUTPUT SET (   10,    1)
OUTPUT VECTOR           1
MACHINE NUMBERS         1    2    4    8    10

INDEX OF INPUT SET  (   10,    1)
PRIMARY INPUT           110
INDEX OF OUTPUT SET (   11,    1)
OUTPUT VECTOR           1
MACHINE NUMBERS         1    2
INDEX OF OUTPUT SET (   11,    2)
OUTPUT VECTOR           0
MACHINE NUMBERS         4    8    10
           CURRENT STRATEGY   BESTNEXT

INDEX OF INPUT SET  (   11,    1)
PRIMARY INPUT           010
INDEX OF OUTPUT SET (   12,    1)
OUTPUT VECTOR           0
MACHINE NUMBERS         1
INDEX OF OUTPUT SET (   12,    2)
OUTPUT VECTOR           1
MACHINE NUMBERS         2
```

Figure 4.13   Final output for fault simulation.

mode are given via the ØPTIØN directive; thus

ØPTIØN

MAINTAIN,SUBSET,2,1,CHECKØUT,WANDER,10,.

set flags which cause the Analyzer to MAINTAIN the present test diagram (rather than starting over at SUBSET,0,0); cause tests to be generated to extend the branch whose current leaf is the equivalence class SUBSET,2,1; select the CHECKØUT figure of merit for test evaluation; and specify that a maximum of 10 random steps are to be taken if the WANDER heuristic is used.

The Analyzer now attempts to generate and simulate a test sequence that will distinguish all of the machines of SUBSET,2,1 from the good machine. These tests are appended to the user's test sequence, yielding the final diagnostic tree of Figures 4.14a–c. The actual system output is given in Figure 4.13. The gross program flow that generates this output is as follows.

Refer to Figure 4.9, where a set of four heuristic programs H_1–H_4 is shown. These are used to generate tests for the subject circuit, and they are simply

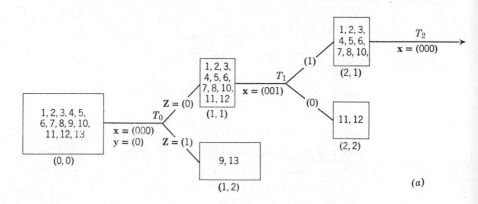

(a)

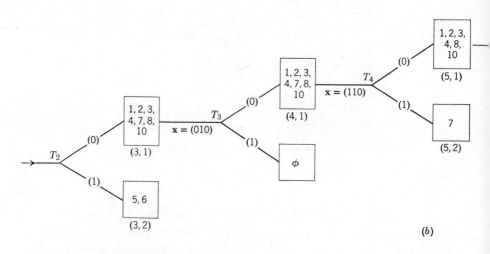

(b)

implementations of the four heuristics discussed in Subsection 3.2.2. The fact that they are not guaranteed to produce useful tests gives rise to the program organization which we now describe. (Some of this organization was sketched in Subsection 3.2.2.)

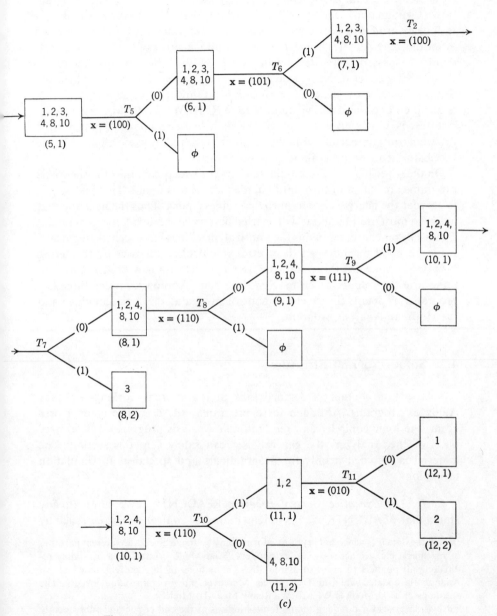

Figure 4.14 Fully grown diagnostic tree for Figure 4.13.

The heuristic programs are ordered arbitrarily, and the first routine is asked to generate a test. It proposes a candidate test (or tests) which is simulated on a trial basis,[7] control being passed from the heuristic program down through bookkeeping to PRØGRAM HUFFMAN. (The actual simulation is done by groups of 48, exactly as was described earlier for MANUAL mode.) After the candidate has been simulated for all machines of the current subset, control is passed to the test evaluation program. This program computes the test's figure of merit by examining the partition of machines which the test produced. If the figure of merit exceeds a threshold value, the candidate is accepted and the Analyzer returns to WRMI (We Really Mean It) Mode. The test is simulated again, all of the data lists are updated, and normal program output occurs. Finally, a usefulness index associated with the successful heuristic program is incremented.

On the other hand, if the candidate test(s) is inadequate, the other heuristic programs are called in turn until an adequate test is found. The final step is to reorder the heuristic programs by usefulness index. Thus the heuristic that has been most useful thus far will be tried first when the next test is generated.[8] The Analyzer continues in this loop until all machines have been distinguished from the good machine.[9] It then returns control to the user by reentering MANUAL mode. At this point, the user may select a new branch and continue in either mode, or he may end the run. We now consider three key programs in detail: the executive control program, the logic compiler and the Huffman Analysis program.

4.3   Some Program Structure

This section contains a detailed look at the internal workings of three Analyzer programs. Although these programs—the executive control program, the logic compiler and the Huffman Analysis program—are primary parts of the Analyzer, the general user can safely skip this section. The material is included mainly for programmers and specialists in simulation technology.

4.3.1   The Executive Control Program READCNTR.   We have already stated that READCNTR's job is to read and obey control directives issued by

---

[7] All of the data lists which hold current information about machine states, present partition of machines, etc. are accessed via list pointers. Trial Mode is established by simply redirecting all pointers to point to dummy lists. Thus none of the "current state" of the Analyzer is updated while in Trial Mode. Moreover, no program output occurs. The antithesis of Trial Mode is WRMI (We Really Mean It) Mode.

[8] Provision exists for dumping the usefulness indices at the end of run and subsequently reloading them. Thus the "learning" process may be carried on from run to run.

[9] It will also stop automatic test generation if all heuristic programs fail to produce an adequate test. This outcome did not occur in the case of EXAMPLE.

the user. Thus, READCNTR permits the user to converse with the Analyzer in a natural, problem-oriented language.

Like most programs of its type, READCNTR has a syntactic phase and a semantic phase. The syntactic phase serves to parse the control directives, and the semantic phase assigns operational meaning to the parsed directives by associating them with subroutines of executable code. The grammar of the Analyzer's control directives is almost trivial. Each directive consists of a sequence of from one to fifteen fields, separated by commas. Each field is a string of from one to eight characters. The first field is special; it is called the *directive identifier*—more on this in a moment. (We shall resist the temptation to write all of this in Backus Normal Form, unorthodox as the use of simple English may be here!)

The semantic phase is equally straightforward. The first field of each directive (the directive identifier) serves to identify the directive with a subroutine of the Analyzer. The subroutine in turn operationally defines the meaning of the control directive. The remaining fields, if any, are used by the subroutine as data, and therefore modify its "meaning" in this sense. A minor complication is introduced by the fact that some subroutines are open whereas others are closed.

This setup gives rise to the following flow of control within READCNTR. The initial entry points for the entire Sequential Analyzer are in READCNTR. When control is sent to one of these to start a run, some initial housekeeping is performed by READCNTR. The input, output, and control media are initialized to their default states, and the host computer's real-time clock is started. Control is then sent to the major loop point in READCNTR, to acquire the user's directives. Each directive is read in, and subjected to syntactic and semantic analysis. The subroutine selected by semantic analysis is then executed, and this major loop is repeated until the run is ended.

The syntactic analysis of each directive is done by subroutine PARAMETR of program READCNTR. PARAMETR is used to scan the directive, break it into fields, and store the fields on the list PARSTR (one field per word, left-justified). The semantic analysis (one blushes to use such a highfalutin term for this simple process) is done by first retrieving the directive identifier from the first word of PARSTR. It is then matched against the members of a list RDCNSTAT of directive identifiers associated with open subroutines. If the jth member of RDCNSTAT yields a match, the jth member of list RDCNSWT1 is retrieved. (This item is the entry address of the open subroutine which is needed.) A simple transfer to this address is executed. Control is eventually returned to the major loop point of READCNTR by the called subroutine.

Alternatively, if no member of RDCNSTAT yields a match, a second list CNTRPRØG of identifiers associated with closed subroutines is searched. The same switching technique is used to activate the proper closed subroutine.

The sole differences here are that the list of addresses is named RDCNSWT2; and that a link transfer, rather than a simple transfer, is used to pass control. In either case, the subroutine may go to PARSTR to retrieve additional (data) fields of the directive.

If no match for the directive identifier is found on either list, the user is reprimanded via the error message medium. The reprimand is followed by either a return to the major loop point, to acquire his next directive (if we are in conversational mode); or by a cut-out to the next job (if we are in batch mode).

To conclude, the entire semantic phase of READCNTR is really nothing but a pair of program switches. This organization was easy to design and debug. It is also well-suited to changes in the repertoire of command directives, as these involve little more than adding items to (or deleting items from) a pair of lists. We now examine the internal structure of the logic compiler.

4.3.2   The Logic Compiler.   First, it will be helpful to review this program's rôle. The compiler feeds on the ØRGANIZEd (partially-ordered) gate declarations of the subject, and puts out a routine capable of simulating both the good subject and the singly-failed subjects. This routine, called the *compiled simulator*, accepts the subject's present state **y** and next primary inputs **X** as inputs; and computes the next feedback outputs **Y** and primary outputs **Z**. Hence the compiled simulator corresponds to the combinational network $\mathscr{C}$ of the Huffman model. This correspondence is illustrated in Figure 4.10.

In addition to the compiled simulator, the logic compiler produces two byproducts. The first is the enumeration of failures for the subject. The second is a set of memory references to a list FAILSIML of failure-injection words. (The failure-injection words are used as data by the compiled simulator. They serve to "inject" s–a–0 and s–a–1 failures into the simulated subject.)

For speed, the simulator processes 48 failed machines at once (parallel simulation). This gives rise to some complications in data layouts, which we now describe. First, the "present state" data for the simulator are *not* a single row vector

$$\mathbf{y};$$

but a $p \times 48$ matrix

$$(\mathbf{y}_1^{\,t}, \mathbf{y}_2^{\,t}, \ldots, \mathbf{y}_{48}^{\,t})$$

of column vectors, having one column for each of the current group of 48 machines, where p denotes the number of feedback variables. Consecutive rows of this matrix are laid out in memory as consecutive words (of 48 bits), so the jth row (word) gives the value of the jth feedback input signal for all

48 of the current machines. This is done to meet the requirements of the compiled simulator, which demands this layout of data.[10]

Second, the "next primary input" datum is a single row vector

$$\mathbf{X}$$

as supplied by the user or heuristic test generator; but it too must be expanded into a matrix

$$(\mathbf{X}^t, \mathbf{X}^t, \ldots, \mathbf{X}^t)$$

of identical column vectors, before the simulator can use it.

Finally, by the same token, the compiled simulator's outputs are actually matrices

$$(\mathbf{Y}_1{}^t, \mathbf{Y}_2{}^t, \ldots, \mathbf{Y}_{48}{}^t),$$

and

$$(\mathbf{Z}_1{}^t, \mathbf{Z}_2{}^t, \ldots, \mathbf{Z}_{48}{}^t),$$

of feedback and primary output vectors.

The simulator is created by compiling a fragment of code for each gate of the subject. The fragment serves to simulate the action of the gate. The fragments are then simply concatenated, in the same order as the ØRGANIZEd gate declarations, to form a simulator. Preservation of the partial ordering imposed by the LØGIC ØRGANIZER allows us to execute the simulator in a single, straight-line pass with no loops or transfers. The correspondence between gate declarations and code fragments is pretty simple, and was illustrated in Figure 4.5 for a two-input AND gate. Thus the logic compiler does a job which is very much like macro expansion. Of course, the code fragments are actually expressed in the Control Data 3600 assembly language —FAP is used in Figure 4.5 because it is a better-known language.

We can also use Figure 4.5 to explain the failure injection words. Suppose that the failure

$$x_1 \text{ to } A1 \text{ open}$$

is the *j*th member of the set of 48 being processed by the simulator. This failure is equivalent to

$$x_1 \text{ s-a-1.}$$

In this case, the *j*th bit of the word at address FAIL1 would be 1; all other bits would be 0. Hence the desired effect, since the gate $A1$ would be simulated with x_1 s-a-1 for the *j*th failure of the current set of 48. Of course, the contents of FAIL1 would change (to all-zeroes) when any other set of failures was being simulated.

[10]An examination of Figure 4.5 shows why this is so. Unfortunately, PRØGRAM HUFFMAN requires that the feedback input and output matrices be transposed. This is done by calling on the routine TRANSPØS, which simultaneously transposes a matrix and moves it to a new work area.

The program flow that results from all of this follows. We enter the compiler at an initialization routine. The count for failure enumeration is set to 2, and the initial instruction[11] is loaded into the compiled simulator. We then go into the major loop which treats each gate declaration. For each declaration, we look up the gate type, and convert this to a key that specifies the appropriate fragment of code. We then match the gate name against a list of previously tested gate names. If a match is found, no failure injection is to be done for this gate. We then enter a subroutine to make up the code fragment, passing the gate type-key code and failures/no failures flag as parameters via the accumulator.

The subroutine has two branches, according to whether failures are or are not to be injected. If not, a simulation fragment without the failure-injection instructions is made up in a work area. It is then moved into the compiled simulator. If failure injection is called for, we first compute the addresses of the failure-injection words in the list FAILSIML. (FAILSIML is a list with one word per failed machine. Failure-injection words are moved in and out of FAILSIML during simulation, to reconfigure the simulator for each group of 48 machines. The addresses in question would be FAIL1, FAIL2, and FAIL3 for the example of Figure 4.5. Failure-injection words for failures *not* being simulated during this pass are set to null values. That is, words used by AND instructions are set to all-ones; and words used by ØR instructions are set to all-zeroes. This does not occur in the example, of course, since it has fewer than 48 failures.) Next, we make up the fragment of code in a work area, by masking in the failure addresses and the other addresses. Then, we move the simulation fragment into the compiled simulator as before. Finally, we make up the information that will be printed later as the enumeration of failures, store it in a buffer, and go back to process the next gate declaration.

When all gates have been compiled, we break out of the main loop. Now there is some housekeeping to be done. First, the instructions that fetch failure-injection words are converted from indexed access to absolute access (for speed). Second, the CDC 3600 has two instructions per word. Therefore we pack the compiled code, two instructions per word. Third, we load the exit instruction as the last word of the compiled simulator, and leave the compiler. We then enter a routine to print the enumeration of failures and we are done.

4.3.3   The Huffman Analysis Program.   The purpose of this Subsection is to describe some structural details of a rather complicated program. The description leans heavily on the basic notions of Huffman Analysis (see Subsection 2.1.1) and on the functions performed by the program in the

---

[11] The compiled simulator is a closed subroutine. The initial instruction provides part of the linkage for transferring back to the calling program (PRØGRAM HUFFMAN).

Sequential Analyzer (see Section 4.2). The reader should be familiar with that material before tackling this subsection; we give a brief summary of it here for completeness.

Basically, PRØGRAM HUFFMAN serves to "close the feedback lines" of a simulated asynchronous circuit. It calls on the compiled simulator as a subroutine. Together, these two programs provide a programmed implementation of the Huffman model for asynchronous circuits. (This is illustrated in Figure 4.10.) PRØGRAM HUFFMAN analyzes 48 machines at once, for compatibility with the compiled simulator. However, there is a major complication in the program because of the following fact.

Normally, the 48 entities simulated by PRØGRAM HUFFMAN and the compiled simulator are machines $M_j, \ldots, M_{j+47}$, which correspond to distinct failures of the subject. (When this is the case, the programs are said to be in *normal mode*.) However, the whole picture changes when a race is discovered. If, for some machine,

$$M_k \in \{M_{j+q}\} \qquad q = 0, 1, \ldots, 47$$

two or more feedback lines are simultaneously unstable, PRØGRAM HUFF-MAN and the simulator are both reconfigured to follow the race branches $\{B_k{}^l\}$ of M_k.[12] The reconfigured programs are said to be in *race analysis mode*.[13]

Reconfiguration is simple for the compiled simulator—we merely alter the contents of FAILSIML so that only M_k's failure is injected. However, reconfiguration of PRØGRAM HUFFMAN is more complicated. The rest of this subsection is devoted to a description of the normal and race analysis modes of operation.

We first describe normal mode. (This was covered in less detail in Section 4.2.) PRØGRAM HUFFMAN receives a primary input vector

$$\mathbf{X}$$

from the user or from an heuristic test generator. It also has a matrix

$$(\mathbf{y}_1{}^t, \mathbf{y}_2{}^t, \ldots, \mathbf{y}_{48}{}^t)^t = \begin{pmatrix} \mathbf{y}_1 \\ \mathbf{y}_2 \\ \cdot \\ \cdot \\ \cdot \\ \mathbf{y}_{48} \end{pmatrix}$$

of present states for the current group of 48 failed machines. These data either came (indirectly) from the user, if a reset was to be simulated, or were computed by transposing the results of the previous input simulation.

---

[12] Here, $B_k{}^l$ denotes the *l*th race branch arising from a race of the *k*th failed machine, M_k.
[13] The procedure used to treat potential oscillations (one unstable feedback line) is much simpler. In this case, both programs remain in normal mode.

A bookkeeping routine is used to expand the primary input vector into a primary input matrix

$$(\mathbf{X}^t, \mathbf{X}^t, \ldots, \mathbf{X}^t)$$

of 48 identical columns. Then the routine TRANSPØS is called, to transpose the feedback input matrix and move it to an input area for the compiled simulator.[14] PRØGRAM HUFFMAN then calls the compiled simulator as a closed subroutine. The simulator computes matrices

$$(\mathbf{Y}_1^t, \mathbf{Y}_2^t, \ldots, \mathbf{Y}_{48}^t)$$

and

$$(\mathbf{Z}_1^t, \mathbf{Z}_2^t, \ldots, \mathbf{Z}_{48}^t),$$

of feedback and primary outputs for the current group of failed machines. Control then returns to PRØGRAM HUFFMAN. The first action taken is to fetch and transpose the feedback output matrix. This again is done by TRANSPØS, which moves the transposed matrix

$$(\mathbf{Y}_1^t, \mathbf{Y}_2^t, \ldots, \mathbf{Y}_{48}^t)^t = \begin{pmatrix} \mathbf{Y}_1 \\ \mathbf{Y}_2 \\ \cdot \\ \cdot \\ \cdot \\ \mathbf{Y}_{48} \end{pmatrix}$$

into a work area for Huffman Analysis. Then, the feedback input and output vectors are compared for each machine. This is done by comparing corresponding rows of

$$\begin{pmatrix} \mathbf{Y}_1 \\ \mathbf{Y}_2 \\ \cdot \\ \cdot \\ \cdot \\ \mathbf{Y}_{48} \end{pmatrix}$$

and the previously saved matrix

$$\begin{pmatrix} \mathbf{y}_1 \\ \mathbf{y}_2 \\ \cdot \\ \cdot \\ \cdot \\ \mathbf{y}_{48} \end{pmatrix}.$$

If $\mathbf{y}_j = \mathbf{Y}_j,$

[14] The matrix is also saved in nontransposed form, for later use in Huffman Analysis.

then the jth machine is stable and needs no further attention. If this is true for all 48 machines, we are done. However, if

$$\mathbf{y}_k \neq \mathbf{Y}_k$$

for some machine M_k, there may be a critical race and/or oscillation. We therefore proceed as follows.

We first go to the major decision point of PRØGRAM HUFFMAN. Here, we count the unstable feedback lines of M_k and act accordingly. Let d_H be the Hamming metric; then, if

(a) $d_H(\mathbf{y}_k, \mathbf{Y}_k) = 0$, M_k is stable and we do not process it any further.
(b) $d_H(\mathbf{y}_k, \mathbf{Y}_k) = 1$, M_k is unstable and may be oscillating.
(c) $d_H(\mathbf{y}_k, \mathbf{Y}_k) \geq 2$, M_k is unstable and a race is in progress.

In this case, outcome (a) is impossible. If (b) occurs, we set a flag HFCYCFLG to indicate that another cycle through the simulator is necessary. We increment the cycle counter and change $\mathbf{y}_k$ to agree with $\mathbf{Y}_k$. (This is done repeatedly if more than one machine M_k has a potential oscillation.) Then we execute the compiled simulator. If outcome (b) continues to occur, we repeat this loop until the cycle count exceeds a threshold value NUMITER (supplied by the user). Then we declare M_k to be oscillating, put out a message to this effect, discard M_k, and return to normal processing. If M_k settles into a stable state before the cycle count has exceeded the threshold value, this whole analysis remains invisible to the user—we set $\mathbf{y}_k$ to the new stable state and go back to normal processing. If outcome (c) occurs, we enter race analysis mode as follows.

First we check to see if we are already in race analysis mode. If we are not (as is the case here), we reconfigure the compiled simulator. To do this, we first save the present states of the current group $\{M_j\}$ of failed machines. This is done by copying the matrix of present states $\mathbf{y}_j$ into a SAVE area. Then we alter the failure injection words in FAILSIML to cause injection of M_k's failure only. All 48 feedback input vectors $\mathbf{y}_j$ are set equal to M_k's state $\mathbf{y}_k$. Then we zero the cycle counter, initialize another counter to indicate that one race branch exists at this point, and initialize various flags.

Next we execute a piece of code which might be called the BRANCH EXPANDER. One feedback input vector $\mathbf{y}_l$ is set up for each branch B_k^l of the race, and the branch counter is incremented accordingly. Simultaneous feedback changes are not considered, on physical grounds. (Thus, if two feedback lines y_m and y_n of M_k were unstable, two input vectors $\mathbf{y}_1$ and $\mathbf{y}_2$ would be modified. The event "y_m changes first" would be simulated by $\mathbf{y}_1$, and the event "y_n changes first" by $\mathbf{y}_2$. The race branch counter would be incremented to value 2.) Now a test is made to determine whether the counter value exceeds 48. If it does, we cannot analyze the race any further. In this case the race is declared critical, and we return to normal mode after dropping M_k and printing an error message.

After leaving the BRANCH EXPANDER, we execute the compiled simulator and then return to the major decision point. However, if outcome (*a*) occurs while we are in race analysis mode, some extra gyrations are necessary. We must consult a flag to see if this branch is the first to settle. If it is, we set the flag and go on. If not, we compare the final states of this branch and the branch that settled previously. If they disagree, a critical race has been found. We therefore print a message to the user and return to normal mode, as described above. If the final states agree, we go on to the next branch.

The overall process continues until the recycle flag HFCYCFLG has been reset, or until one of the reasons for termination listed above occurs. If the former is the case, all race branches have settled in the same final state, so the race was noncritical. Here, no message occurs and the entire process remains invisible to the user. We return to normal mode by restoring the simulator and executing a routine HFRCNRML to switch PRØGRAM HUFFMAN.

It seems appropriate to close this subsection with a quote from Seshu (1964): "Modifications to this routine are not advisable."

4.4   Analyzer Applications

This section discusses some problems that have been attacked with the help of the Sequential Analyzer. We first deal with straightforward applications and then move on to a more complex problem: computer self-diagnosis. The section closes with a critique of the present Analyzer, based on the experience gained from these studies.

4.4.1   Straightforward Applications.   Here, we outline some trial studies done at Bell Telephone Laboratories, aimed at development of factory test methods for integrated circuitry and improvement of certain computer diagnostic procedures.

Integrated circuit (IC) technology has provided logic circuits that have from two to several hundred gates in a single substrate of semiconductor. However, test access is obviously limited to the circuit primary inputs and outputs. Furthermore, the logic design must be free of errors before production of the circuit begins, since the cost of correcting a design error after production has begun may be very high.

Both problems have been attacked with the Analyzer. The coded circuit description of an IC chip was made up, with the appropriate input and output declarations, and a fault detection sequence was generated. Design errors have been found by examining the simulated good machine behavior, and the test sequence could be incorporated into the factory test equipment.

However, the Analyzer does not simulate all possible failure modes of many types of IC chips, and this approach has not yet been widely accepted throughout Bell Telephone Laboratories. Nevertheless, it seems to us to be very promising, particularly for chips having several hundred gates and many feedback loops which are expected in the near future.

The Analyzer has also been applied (on a very limited scale) to the problem of improving diagnosis procedures for the No. 1 Electronic Switching System. These procedures were generated manually and simulated by the method of physical fault simulation. As we pointed out in Section 3.4, this approach often results in certain faults going undetected. The Analyzer has been used to simulate small portions of the machine having undetected faults, leading to supplementary tests which were then used to improve the diagnostic procedures. In one case, a 64-gate adder having 14 undetected faults was treated, and supplementary tests for all of these faults were produced by the Analyzer.

4.4.2 Research in Computer Self-Diagnosis. This study constitutes probably the most elaborate application of the Sequential Analyzer to date. As the title imples, the problem was to derive techniques that would allow an unduplicated processor to perform checkout and diagnosis of itself. [It was this absence of duplication that distinguished the problem from other studies in the literature. See, for instance, Downing et al. (1964), or Forbes et al. (1965).] The description given here is largely a summary of published articles by Manning (1966a, 1966b).

A nearly complete absence of insight at the beginning of the study dictated an experimental approach. Thus an attempt was made to derive a self-diagnosis procedure for the hardware used in executing instructions (control, arithmetic unit, and decoders) of an existing computer. The subject chosen was the CSX-1,[15] a small, asynchronous machine. It was hoped that the experiment would yield sufficient insight to allow the formulation of design principles leading to more diagnosable computers.

A self-diagnosis procedure was defined as a procedure having exactly two possible outcomes:

1. The execution-phase hardware is entirely failure free.
2. Card or module x has a fault of type y.

Furthermore, the procedure must be simple enough to permit execution several times per day. (We must do this in order to validate the single-fault assumption.) Notice that we permit the use of an unskilled human operator, and we do allow the machine to go out of service while being diagnosed and

---

[15] The CSX-1 has been described by Manning (1966a) and by Brown et al. (1964).

repaired. Hence the results are more directly relevant to batch-processing installations than to real-time systems.[16]

The Sequential Analyzer was the principal experimental tool. As in the simpler applications described previously, the Analyzer was used to simulate the circuit of interest. However, in this case, the circuit of interest was a large part of a digital processor, comprising about 700 AND-OR-NOT macrogates and having 5200 failures. Of course, all of the assumptions underlying the Analyzer (see Section 4.1) were also relevant to this study. We now describe the experimental approaches that were tried.

Several approaches based on well-known ideas were tried and rejected. First, an attempt was made to specify and manually check a portion of the hardware that could serve as a tester.[17] The tester portion could then be used to check the rest of the hardware. However, the number of manual tests required was prohibitive, even in the case of the CSX-1. Next, a more involved approach was tried. It was assumed that a set S of instructions capable of simulating all other instructions would have to be tested somehow, before execution of any complex instruction could be usefully attempted. Otherwise, no method of evaluating the outcome of the execution would be available. (The assumption, although widely held, is false.)

This approach led to very lengthy diagnosis procedures, due to the long sequences of S-instructions required. Finally, it was realized that *the use of the Analyzer allowed one to determine the effect of every machine failure on any instruction.* Hence one can start diagnosis by simply attempting to execute any instruction. The possible results, no matter how bizarre, can all be predicted in advance by simulation. Thus the falsity of the assumption stated above, and thus the procedure that we now describe.

Each instruction of the procedure was chosen to utilize as many previously unused microinstructions as possible.[18] As a secondary criterion, each instruction was chosen to exercise as many new ordered pairs of microinstructions as possible. Since microinstructions of the CSX-1 correspond one-to-one with the control points of the control, and ordered pairs correspond to the interface circuitry between control points, these criteria locally maximize the information gain at each step. Thus the procedure is more efficient than the ones yielded by the approach discussed in Section 3.4. However, because of the absence of global optimization, the results may not be optimal. Parenthetically, notice that Seshu's heuristics are suboptimal for the same reasons.

---

[16] They can easily be extended, however, by methods discussed in the sequel.

[17] The properties of a tester were outlined in Section 2.3.

[18] This method of manual test generation may be compared with the method described in Section 3.4.

The input and output vectors for simulation were taken to be the directed cutsets between the execution-phase hardware and the rest of the CSX-1. Two global feedback lines were broken to allow the simulated control to reach stable states. Hence each CSX-1 instruction was simulated as a sequence of approximately 30 primary inputs.

At each input applied, the Analyzer of course partitioned the class of failed machines with respect to output vectors. We could continue to simulate the execution of CSX-1 instructions until all distinguishable machines had been partitioned. The resulting sequence of CSX-1 instructions would be called the *cutset-basis checkout sequence.*[19] Observe that we are selecting a sequence of tests here, and then we are asking the Analyzer to enumerate the faults detected. This approach is also found in the strategy routines, and is in contradistinction to procedures such as the *d*-algorithm where a test is generated for a specific fault.

Now the failed machines may behave in any of several ways. We must convert all possible behaviors into some sort of standard form, which a human operator can recognize and interpret easily. We do this as follows. Even the most inexperienced and badly motivated of operators should be able to tell whether a processor is running or stopped. Moreover, he should be able to make observations about the state of a stopped processor from the console displays. We therefore specify that *every processor fault shall cause the processor to stop prematurely* while executing the self-diagnosis procedure.[20] We attempt to meet this requirement as follows.

1. A failed machine may enter a stable state because of the fault involved. In this case, which is common for an asynchronous machine but rare for a clocked one, no further effort is necessary. This case is identified during simulation by analysis of the sequence of output vectors produced. Furthermore, we associate the stable state entered under failure with the particular set of failures, with the help of the simulator output.

2. A failed machine may complete all instructions but produce a wrong result in one of the registers. In this case we append a string of instructions to the procedure which will cause a programmed stop. It is also necessary to simulate the string for the subset of machines in question, to ensure that the failures involved do not incapacitate any instructions of the string itself. This case is also identified during simulation by analysis of output vectors (all machine register contents can be deduced from the output vectors).

---

[19] In fact, the experiment was stopped before all distinguishable machines had been partitioned. This was mostly because of acute fatigue on the part of the experimenter.

[20] Thus the use of multiple processors, each capable of detecting a stopped state of the others (via a "dead-man switch" using a timer), would suffice to extend these results to real-time systems.

The contents of the program counter in the stopped machine can be used by the operator to identify the failures involved.[21]

3. The outcome of the self-diagnosis procedure may not exist or may not be unique. These cases, which are respectively due to oscillations or critical races induced by failure, are identified by the Huffman Analysis Program of the Analyzer. No adequate treatment was provided for these cases, and the machines involved are simply discarded after identification.

4. The behavior of a failed machine may be identical to the good machine's behavior over the entire procedure. That is, it may be impossible to find a test sequence that detects the failure. In this case the failure is redundant, and redesign of the circuitry involved is called for. We now discuss the results that this experiment produced.

Table 4.1   Experimental Statistics

Column	1	2	3	4	5	6	7	8
Adder & control	1142	160	972	866	57	27	125	2239
Decoders	793	~	602	507	79	357	124	1519
Totals	1935	160	1574	1373	136	384	249	3758

Legend.

Column 1, Number of machines causing hangup.
2, Subset of (1) due to adder failures.
3, Number of machines not causing hangup.
4, Subset of (3) which cause obvious changes in contents of some register, and therefore can be detected easily by programming.
5, Subset of (3), which can be detected by a checking circuit on request lines, that is, machines generating several simultaneous requests.
6, Subset of (3) which can be detected by a checking circuit on switch selector lines.
7, Number of machines of unknown behavior.
8, Total number of well-behaved machines partitioned.

In order to perform the experiment, the 5200 failures of the CSX-1 execution hardware had to be split into two classes, and treated in two separate simulations. For both failure classes, the number of failed machines distinguished from the good machine is given as a function of the number of instructions executed (Figure 4.15). The asymptotic behavior of the curves is a phenomenon that several workers have observed.

[21] Alternatively, the techniques of Chapter V could be used to translate the simulation data into repair information.

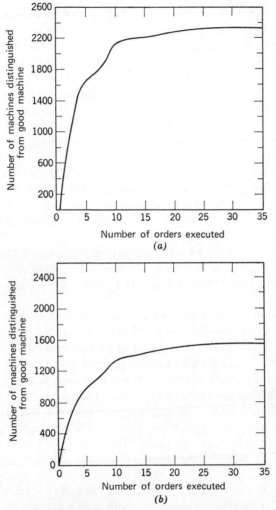

Figure 4.15 Rates of partitioning. (*a*) Adder and control failures. (*b*) Decoder failures. Note: Order No. 1 is the action "reset all feedback lines."

After 33 CSX-1 instructions had been simulated once each, the final partition of machines obtained was examined. At this point, 83 percent of the control and arithmetic unit failures and 61 percent of the decoder failures had been detected. Some features of the final partition are given in Table 4.1. Notice that the majority of the *well-behaved failures* (those failures that do not cause oscillations or critical races) cause the machine to stop. About 86 percent of the remaining failures cause an obvious change in the contents of some machine register. For the remaining well-behaved failures (about 7 percent), it was impossible to predict the behavior of the computer. This was because of the bizarre output vectors sent to the remainder of the CSX-1, calling for such things as simultaneous execution of multiply and divide operations, simultaneous fetching and execution of instructions, and many other operations never intended in the original design of the subject. This problem could be partially resolved by simulating the entire processor as one circuit, if a digital fault simulator of sufficient speed and capacity were available. Finally, the number of failure-induced oscillations and critical races was extremely small. Thus the existence and uniqueness of the result of self-diagnosis was not a severe problem.

Manning (1966a) gives an estimate of the total length of the self-diagnosis procedure for the CSX-1 execution hardware. This was found to be 7000 instructions, requiring 70 milliseconds for their execution. Thus the execution time was acceptably small. We now give a summary of the design principles extracted from the study.

The principles summarized here vary in level from circuit design to rather general system principles. They were all suggested by experience gained from the experimental study, and are described more thoroughly in Manning (1966b).

Turning first to general principles, a diagnosable computer should be asynchronous and sequential mode. (That is, the request and reply signals should be d-c levels, rather than pulses as in a pulse mode machine.) This type of realization maximizes the number of failures which cause the machine to stop, and also reduces malfunction due to timing problems. Second, a diagnosable machine should be free of redundant logic, unless that logic can be rendered nonredundant for testing. The reason is simply that faults of redundant logic cannot in general be detected, thus invalidating the single-fault assumption. Third, the diagnosis procedure should be produced concurrently with the design of the subject. (This point was discussed in Section 3.4.)

With respect to the circuit level, we notice that failure-induced oscillations and critical races hamper self-diagnosis, both in denying existence or uniqueness to the outcome of the self-diagnosis procedure, and in increased production costs incurred by Huffman analysis. Hence one would like to minimize these unpleasant phenomena. We note that noncritical races of the CSX-1 processor were observed to become critical under failure; therefore, totally sequential realizations are suggested. (Such realizations also reduce production cost, since every noncritical race required extensive Huffman analysis.) Second, strong connectedness is advocated. For if a machine possesses *unreachable states* (states that are never entered by the failure-free machine when started from its normal reset state), they may be entered under failure. This happened frequently with the CSX-1, and was the root cause of the machines of unknown outcome mentioned previously. As strong connectedness is a sufficient condition for the nonexistence of unreachable states, our recommendation follows. Third, circuits of short *transient length* are suggested. (The transient length of a circuit is K iff the maximum number of state-transitions between pairs of stable states is K.) A result has been established which shows, roughly, that the number of failures which create oscillations increases with the transient length of the circuit.

Finally, on the system level, a well-modularized design is advocated as an aid to partitioning and as a measure to localize strange behavior caused by failures. Control modules which stop upon receiving illegal sequences are obviously useful (the CSX-1 control has this property). A minimal number of global feedback loops has also been found to be of value.

Now the obvious next step, after an experimental study leading to design principles, is to reenter the design cycle and see if the principles advocated do in fact yield "better" designs. The study described by Manning (1966b) did not take this final step. However, the design principles given above have been largely observed in an exploratory project in telephone switching processor design at Bell Telephone Laboratories. Consequently, results on the diagnosability of such designs may be available in the not-too-distant future.

The Analyzer Applications just discussed represent a sizeable amount of experience gained in the use of the Sequential Analyzer. This experience has led us to form some strong opinions about the strengths and weaknesses of the present Analyzer. These views are summarized in the next subsection.

4.4.3 Critique of the Sequential Analyzer. In reading this material, the reader might bear in mind that the Sequential Analyzer has been used in a variety of applications, many of which were not anticipated by the Sequential Analyzer's designer. Thus many of the shortcomings experienced clearly do not reflect discredit on the original design decisions. Nonetheless, critical reviews of any system are essential to further improvement, and the present Analyzer is no exception to this rule. The principal deficiencies we have found are in speed, capacity, modeling, failure modes, and automatic test generation. We now examine these deficiencies in turn.

Digital fault simulation has many advantages as a tool for verifying processor diagnostics and generating fault simulation data, as we suggested in Section 3.4. However, this application requires the simulation of all or most of a processor as one circuit; and the present Analyzer (CDC 3600 implementation) would require more than 3×10^3 hours to do the job, for a medium-scale processor of 10^4 gates. Hence the speed of simulation is quite inadequate for this prime application. The present capacities of 3×10^3 logic gates and 5×10^3 faults are also a bit off the mark. The most severe inadequacy, however, is the limit of the 48 feedback loops, which is at least an order of magnitude below the requirements for processor simulation.

Concerning modelling, we recall that the Analyzer employs the simplest Huffman model of a sequential circuit. Now this is reasonably adequate for asynchronous sequential-mode circuitry, and we have pointed out that such realizations facilitate self-diagnosis. (This indeed was one reason for the original choice of the Huffman model.) Nevertheless, a general-purpose fault simulator must be able to handle a much wider class of realizations. Asynchronous sequential-mode circuitry is rare in today's designs. The vast majority is pulse-mode and usually clocked. Critical races are commonly introduced by the designers to simplify design and save components. Worse yet, there are many clocked designs that do not even obey the classical rules for synchronous logic—some feedback loops are unclocked, and the clock pulse is left on in other loops for a long enough period to allow them to behave asynchronously. Finally, it is quite common for ten or more feedback loops to simultaneously change state, which constitutes a race of 2^{10} or more branches. This of course violates the restriction on the number of race branches allowed. None of these designs can be meaningfully simulated by the present Sequential Analyzer.

Turning to failure modes, we have found that the "open input diode" and "gate outputs stuck" modes are handled reasonably well for discrete transistor-diode circuitry. The simulation of shorted diodes is inadequate, due to nonlogical effects which these failures can introduce into the physical circuits.[22] Finally, the topic of failure modelling of integrated circuits is an open question. We are aware both of IC failure modes which the present Analyzer can handle well, and of new modes which will demand a more powerful method.

The heuristics described in Section 3.2 have proved to be reasonably effective in generating tests for small circuits. However, they are often impractical for large circuits because of the quantities of host computer time required to simulate the various candidate tests. Furthermore, the COMBINATIONAL heuristic, based on an early form of one-dimensional path sensitizing, has become obsolete with the advent of better methods (see Section 3.1). Thus there is considerable room for improvement in the automatic test generation facility.

We have also noted that the present strategy routines employ local rather than global optimization techniques; therefore, they do not guarantee a minimal test sequence. This contrasts with the work of Poage (truly minimal sequences), which we have described. However, we feel that this shortcoming is largely of only academic concern. Memory devices have been getting steadily cheaper, and this trend is likely to accelerate. Also, there are very few computer applications in which a few extra milliseconds required to diagnose a fault constitutes a crucial issue. Hence we see no great need to reduce the amount of time and storage required for testing to an absolute minimum.

[22] Chang (1969) has described new simulation techniques for dealing with such faults.

In the balance, these criticisms must be weighed against the many advantages offered by digital fault simulation. Our judgement, based on the arguments of Section 3.4, is that digital fault simulation has already become an indispensable tool, but will be even more valuable when these shortcomings have been overcome. Some preliminary studies aimed at correcting these deficiencies are discussed in Section 6.1.

CHAPTER V

Fault Dictionaries

5.1 Introduction

In Section 3.4, we discussed a number of methods for proceeding from faults of a digital system to the corresponding symptoms. We now examine the inverse problem: given a set of symptoms, identify the fault(s) that could be responsible for them. This is the problem that the maintenance man must face in the field (in fact, it is really the central problem of this book); therefore, it is one of practical interest.

All of the methods discussed in Section 3.4 used some sort of simulation technique (indeed, we have called the symptoms *simulation data*), and all of them rested on several key assumptions. The inverse problem is conceptually trivial—we merely invert the mapping obtained from fault simulation—*if* all of the underlying assumptions are in fact valid. Unfortunately, they usually are not.

For example, many subject systems lack adequate reset facilities. This means that the *test results*, obtained by executing a diagnosis procedure in the field, may disagree with the outcome predicted by the simulation data. Moreover, two consecutive executions of a procedure, in the presence of a single, solid fault, may yield test results that do not agree. In other words, the test results may not be reproducible. (We use the term *mismatch* for the first possibility and the term *inconsistency* for the second.) Again, "forbidden" faults[1] may occur in the field, resulting in mismatches. Finally, field maintenance is often done by relatively unskilled people. The sheer volume and complexity of test results and simulation data make them unsuitable tools for such people. Hence, they must be processed to yield compressed, intelligible repair information.

---

[1] "Forbidden" faults were defined in Subsection 2.3.2 as faults that do occur in the field, but were not considered when the diagnosis procedures were generated or simulated. We also noted in Subsection 2.3.2, that the higher redundancy inherent in combinational procedures makes them better suited to handling such faults. For this reason, the exclusive use of combinational testing procedures is assumed throughout this chapter.

In this chapter we put forward the idea of *fault dictionary* as a possible solution to all of these problems. Several techniques for processing simulation data to produce fault dictionaries are discussed. The simplest kind of fault dictionary, the *exact-match dictionary*, is described in Section 5.2, together with a list of its deficiencies. These deficiencies make it necessary to develop more elaborate kinds of dictionaries, which are frequently used as back-ups to an exact-match dictionary. Two kinds of back-up dictionary—the *test phase dictionary* and the *cell dictionary*—are described in Section 5.3. We conclude the chapter with a discussion of comparisons and trade-offs among these techniques (Section 5.4).

5.2   Exact-Match Dictionaries

The exact-match dictionary is the simplest type of fault dictionary. It is basically nothing more than a rearrangement of the simulation data to form a *fault table*. (Fault tables were discussed in Subsection 3.3.1.) It is used in the field in the following manner. The maintenance man first executes the diagnosis procedures, and thus obtains the test results. He then attempts to manually match the observed test results against entries of the dictionary. An exact match serves to identify the fault. This technique is simple and, when it is successful, it allows a relatively unskilled person to diagnose faults within minutes. We now discuss various methods of representing simulation data as an exact-match dictionary.

5.2.1   Straightforward Representations.   If the number of diagnostic tests is small, the straightforward *pass-or-fail representation* may be used. The simulation data for the ith fault f_i are represented by a binary vector

$$\mathbf{f}_i = (f_{i1}, f_{i2}, \ldots, f_{im})$$

where

$$f_{ik} = 1 \quad \text{if } f_i \text{ is detected by test } T_k$$
$$= 0 \quad \text{otherwise}$$

The binary fault vectors are then sorted in descending order (for example), to permit easy reference by the maintenance man. The resulting dictionary looks something like the one shown in Table 5.1. In this representation, the simulation data for the failure-free subject and for all undetected faults are represented by the all-zeroes vector.

Another straightforward representation can be done by recording entire circuit output vectors in the dictionary rather than binary "pass-or-fail" information. This type of representation was illustrated in Table 2.5. In general, this representation provides better diagnostic resolution at the expense of a bulkier dictionary and more difficult look-up. This point was

Table 5.1 Pass-or-Fail
Representation of an
Exact-Match Dictionary

	T_1	T_2	T_3	T_4
f_9	1	1	1	1
f_3	1	1	1	0
f_2	1	1	0	0
f_7	1	0	0	1
f_8	0	1	1	0
f_{10}	0	1	0	0
f_1	0	0	1	0
f_5	0	0	0	1

illustrated by Table 2.5, where machines M_2 and M_3 are distinguishable. However, if a "pass-or-fail" representation had been used, both machines would correspond to the binary vector

$$(0, 0, 1)$$

and would therefore be indistinguishable.

Finally, we may choose to list only the failing tests for each fault. This method is attractive when, on the average, a fault is detected by only a small fraction of the set of tests. The tests are numbered, and the dictionary entries are ordered by the numbers of failing tests. This is shown in Table 5.2, which is derived from Table 5.1. This type of representation was first used commercially as the exact-match dictionary for an experimental electronic switching system. [See Tsiang and Ulrich (1962) for a description.] It is

Table 5.2 Exact-Match
Dictionary Represented by
Failing Test Numbers

Faults	Failing Test Numbers
f_2	1, 2
f_3	1, 2, 3
f_9	1, 2, 3, 4
f_7	1, 4
f_{10}	2
f_8	2, 3
f_1	3
f_5	4
.	.
.	.
.	.

well-suited to manual diagnosis of faults, when no exact match can be found. This is because the set of tests that should fail is explicitly given. Hence one can often examine the field test results with the aid of logic diagrams and program listings in order to analyze any discrepancies.

All of the straightforward representations suffer from two shortcomings: (1) the dictionary is bulky whenever the test set is large (say, in excess of 1000 tests), and (2) the table look-up procedure is lengthy and tiresome whenever there are many failing tests. The representation that we describe next attempts to overcome these difficulties.

5.2.2 The Pseudo-Random Number Representation. The problem here is to reduce drastically the volume and complexity of the dictionary without affecting diagnostic resolution. One approach, used in the No. 1 Electronic Switching System (Downing et al., 1964; Chang and Thomis, 1967), grew from the following observation. The binary fault vectors of the simulation data usually only sparsely populate the space to which they belong. Hence it should be possible to map them into a much "smaller" space with little or no loss of information. This led to the use of a pseudo-random mapping into a set of sequences of decimal integers.[2] The sequences of decimal integers were then sorted to produce a dictionary, which is partially illustrated in Figure 5.1. Of course, the same pseudo-random mapping must be performed

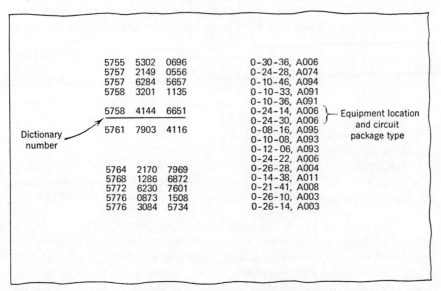

Figure 5.1 Exact-match dictionary represented by pseudo-random numbers.

[2] The mapping was deterministic, but used a well-known procedure to approximate the process of assigning a random number to each fault vector.

on the test results generated in the field before they can be compared with the dictionary entries.

To use such a technique successfully, care must be taken that the diagnostic resolution of the dictionary is not degraded too much. This problem can be dealt with by enlarging the target set of decimal sequences or by improving the "randomness" of the mapping. In the case of the No. 1 ESS, a cut-and-try approach was taken. Both factors were varied, and the resulting diagnostic resolution was evaluated. This process was continued until no further improvement in diagnostic resolution could be obtained. The final product was a dictionary of 12-digit decimal sequences, which provided a five-to-one reduction in dictionary bulk. A detailed account of this development has been given by Chang and Thomis (1967).

5.2.3 Critique of Exact-Match Dictionaries.   We may begin by reviewing the difficulties that fault dictionaries are supposed to overcome. These are: mismatches, inconsistencies, and excessive volume and complexity of the simulation data. Of these, only the last difficulty has been dealt with by exact-match representations. Furthermore, mismatches and inconsistencies can be a major barrier to automated fault diagnosis. For example, experimental data from the No. 1 ESS project suggest that 15 to 20 percent of field diagnoses by exact-match techniques may fail because of these two causes. If the maintenance personnel are obliged to rely exclusively on dictionaries (due to lack of skills and detailed knowledge of the subject), this is clearly an unacceptable state of affairs.

As we have suggested, there are many possible root causes of inconsistency or mismatch. Some of these are as follows.

1. "Forbidden" faults, most notably intermittent, marginal, and non-logical faults.
2. Lack of adequate reset facilities.
3. Electrical noise.
4. Inadequacy of the model used in fault simulation of the subject. (Obviously this could cause discrepancies between the behavior under failure predicted by simulation and the actual behavior observed in the field.)

To sum up; the first three causes of inconsistency or mismatch result from failures to design a diagnosable system. (Some approaches to diagnosable design are outlined in Sections 3.4 and 4.4.) However, a fundamental solution would call for major redesign of the subject, even if a complete set of principles of diagnosable design were available. The fourth cause can be viewed in two ways, depending on the reader's prejudice. It is either a failure of the system designers (to design a system well-suited to available simulation models) or a failure of the simulation programmers (to devise an adequate simulation model for the given subject). In any event, a fundamental solution here, too, would require major developmental effort.

The choice implied is not attractive. One either embarks on a lengthy, expensive developmental program, or one accepts a 15 to 20 percent failure of the automated maintenance procedures. Some kind of interim solution is clearly needed. We now describe several attempts at such a solution.

5.3   Backup Techniques

Our problem is to deal with dictionary mismatches and inconsistencies without altering either the design of the subject or the available simulation data. One approach is to develop flexible ways of interpreting the given simulation data, in the hope that mismatches and inconsistencies can somehow be masked out. It is clear that the success of this approach will depend strongly on the nature of the simulation data at hand. Thus interpretation methods that are effective for one subject may fail miserably when applied to another.

In this section, we first examine the characteristics of the No. 1 ESS simulation data. We then show how these led naturally to a number of data interpretation methods. Although the methods themselves are *ad hoc* and heavily oriented toward the No. 1 ESS, the general approach taken here may be applicable to other systems.

5.3.1   Observed Characteristics of the No. 1 ESS Simulation Data.   An experiment was conducted to study dictionary mismatches. Basically, this involved a comparison of simulation data and test results for some set of faults. (Let us call the bit-by-bit EXCLUSIVE-OR of the fault vectors, obtained from simulation data and field test results, the *mismatch vector* of a fault. Then the experiment was really a study of the mismatch vectors of a sample of subject faults.) The simulation data were already available; the test results were generated by inserting a sample of faults, randomly selected from each subsystem of the subject, into a machine installed in the field. The experiment, which was reported by Chang and Thomis (1967), gave the following results.

(*a*) About 15 to 20 percent of the sample of faults produced nonzero mismatch vectors (i.e., dictionary mismatches).

(*b*) About 75 percent of the nonzero mismatch vectors had only a few nonzero bits. More precisely, less than 1 percent of the bits of these vectors were nonzero. However, many of the remaining 25 percent of mismatch vectors had a large fraction of nonzero bits.

(*c*) The fault vectors were ordered so that adjacent bits represented tests designed for adjacent portions of the subject's hardware. When this was done, the nonzero bits of mismatch vectors tended to appear in clusters. A given mismatch vector might have several such clusters of nonzero bits, but the total set of such bits usually represented less than 1 percent of the mismatch vector.

(*d*) The nonzero bits of the mismatch vectors usually resulted from tests that detected a fault, according to the field test results, but that did not detect it according to the simulation data.

These observations are highly qualitative. However, they suggest a number of *ad hoc* interpretation techniques which we now describe. First, observations (*b*) and (*c*) indicate that a dictionary match could be achieved if the clusters of mismatch bits somehow could be masked out. This idea leads to the *test phase dictionary*. It also suggests the possibility of defining a measure of geometric "nearness" between fault vectors, which would allow us to associate a fault vector of field results with the "nearest" vector from simulation. This notion is the basis of the *cell dictionary*.

5.3.2   The Test Phase Dictionary.   The essential idea here is to partition the total set of tests into *phases*. Each phase consists of the tests that are aimed at a particular portion of the subject, such as a decoder or a sequencer.

An analysis of test results showed that the failing tests are generally distributed over a *very* small subset of the test phases [Chang and Thomis (1967), Kruskal and Hart (1966)]. This result is natural, since one expects a fault to be detected primarily by the tests that were designed to detect it.[3] Hence if we represented the test results as a fault table, we would obtain a table having the general form shown in Figure 5.2. The shaded areas of this figure represent the detection of faults by tests. For example, the shading indicates that f_i has failed certain tests of phases 2, 3, 4, and 6, but has passed all tests of all other phases.

This characteristic of test results has been exploited as follows. In addition to the usual exact match dictionary, we prepare a test phase dictionary. This is composed of many subdictionaries, each of which is created by processing the simulation data of *one test phase*. This setup implies redundant identification of a fault: it would correspond to one entry of the exact-match dictionary and one entry of each of several phase subdictionaries. For example, the fault f_i of Figure 5.2 would be identified by an entry in the exact-match dictionary, plus an entry in each of the phase subdictionaries corresponding to test phases 2, 3, 4, and 6.

Now suppose that f_i of Figure 5.2 occurs in the field, and its test results are

[3] The more modular the design of the subject is, the better this expectation will be borne out by experience.

Test phases ⟶

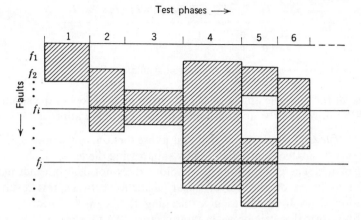

Figure 5.2 Test results arranged by test phases.

obtained by diagnosis. An exact-match dictionary number, as well as four phase subdictionary numbers, will be generated. (The latter numbers are each generated by processing the results from *one* test phase, of course.) The maintenance man will normally try to find a match in the exact-match dictionary. If he succeeds, the fault is immediately known. If not, he can try to match each phase subdictionary number with the entries of the corresponding subdictionary. This procedure gives us some ability to deal with mismatches. For example, some of the tests of test phase 3 may cause a mismatch for f_i. In this case, the third subdictionary will be of no help in identifying f_i. However, if these are the only invalid tests in the diagnosis procedure, the second, fourth, and sixth phase subdictionaries will all yield matches. Since f_i will be listed, possibly together with other sets of faults, at all three entries, it can be readily identified. However, the diagnostic resolution will suffer because of the loss of information that should have been supplied by test phase 3. Therefore, the inconsistency has been suppressed at the expense of additional effort in doing dictionary look-ups plus a possible loss of some diagnostic resolution.

The test phase approach is also helpful in treating intermittent faults. The maintenance man can call for repeated execution of a few phases, hopefully leading to correct diagnosis. It is often impractical to repeat the entire diagnosis procedure many times because of lengthy running times. Moreover, the probability of an intermittent fault remaining "on" during an entire diagnosis obviously increases as the procedure is made shorter.

On the other hand, the test phase approach has two notable shortcomings: (1) if the fault causes mismatches in all test phases that detect the fault, diagnosis is impossible; and (2) the test phase dictionary is usually bulkier

	T_1	T_2	T_3	T_4	T_5	T_6	T_7	T_8	T_9	T_{10}
$\mathbf{f}_i =$	0	0	1	1	0	0	0	1	0	0
$\mathbf{f}_j =$	0	1	1	0	0	1	0	0	0	0

Figure 5.3   Vectors of simulation data.

because of the multiple appearances that each fault makes in the subdiction-aries.[4] We now describe an alternative to the test phase approach.

5.3.3   *The Cell Dictionary.*   The test phase dictionary technique attempts to convert mismatches into matches by suppressing the tests which produced the mismatch. The cell dictionary technique does not deal in exact matches at all; it is based on the use of "near" matches between test results and simulation data. In order to give meaning to the word "near," we first establish a formal metric between fault vectors. We then attempt to use this metric by identifying a vector of test results with the nearest vector of simulation data.

Our development is best illustrated with an example. Consider the vectors of simulation data shown in Figure 5.3. Suppose that f_i is diagnosed in the field, yielding the vector of test results

$$\mathbf{f}'_i = (0, 0, 1, 0, 0, 0, 0, 1, 0, 0)$$

which mismatches $\mathbf{f}_i$. However, $\mathbf{f}_i$ is nearer to $\mathbf{f}'_i$ than to $\mathbf{f}_j$, in the sense of the Hamming distance.[5] This therefore suggests the use of the Hamming metric, which in turn suggests a geometric interpretation of fault vectors. We conceive of N-bit fault vectors as points in the N-dimensional space over the binary field. Now suppose that a vector of test results is placed at point x in this N-space (see Figure 5.4). If x is already occupied by a vector of simulation data, an exact match exists. If not, it seems plausible that the points a_1, a_2, and a_3 of simulation data, which are nearest with respect to the Hamming metric, would represent probable faults. This hypothesis, which is supported by satisfactory results in practice, therefore gives the maintenance man a list of faults to repair. Moreover, the list can be ordered by the corresponding distances, so that the most probable faults can be checked first.

Now that we have defined a metric and have shown how to use it to interpret test results, we must find a representation for the dictionary entries which facilitates the matching process. This is done by conceptually partitioning the N-space into disjoint cells C_i. Each cell has a point c_i of the space as its center. We then associate every point x_k of the space with the cell C_i

---

[4] The bulk tends to increase proportionally to the average number of failing phases per fault.

[5] The Hamming distance between two binary numbers is defined to be the number of corresponding bit positions which differ in value.

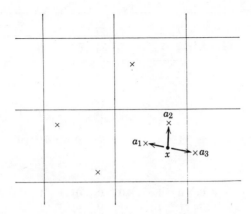

Figure 5.4 Geometric representation of fault vectors in an N-dimensional space.

which minimizes the Hamming distance between x_k and c_i,

$$d_H(x_k, c_i).$$

All of this can be applied to dictionary construction by agreeing that each cell center c_i identifies all faults corresponding to vectors of simulation data which lie within C_i. The cell centers can be defined in a way that permits rapid look-up as follows. We divide an N-bit vector into q segments, and stipulate that all bits in a given segment are identical. The set of such vectors is taken as our cell centers. They clearly define a partition of N-space into 2^q cells of equal "size." We can rapidly determine the cell that contains a given vector simply by counting the numbers of 0s and 1s in each segment. This is because a vector having more 0s (1s) than 1s (0s) in the ith segment is closer with respect to Hamming distance to a cell center whose ith segment contains all 0s (1s). The cell dictionary is therefore nothing but a list of centers of occupied cells, together with the names of the faults that occupy them. There is, of course, no need to list the centers of the cells that contain none of the vectors of simulation data.

An example of the construction of a cell dictionary is given in Figure 5.5a. Each vector is divided into three 3-bit segments. Faults f_i, f_{i+1}, and f_j are assigned to cell

$$000 \quad 000 \quad 111 \quad \text{(or 001, for short)},$$

since their vectors are closest to this center. This process yields the partial dictionary of Figure 5.5b. If a field diagnosis of f_{i+1} subsequently yields

$$\mathbf{f}'_{i+1} = (0, 0, 0, 1, 0, 0, 1, 1, 0),$$

a mismatch exists. However, this vector points to cell 001, which in turn points to faults f_i, f_{i+1} and f_j. Hence we obtain a valid diagnosis.

Faults	S_1			S_2			S_3		
	T_1	T_2	T_3	T_4	T_5	T_6	T_7	T_8	T_9
.				.					
.				.					
.				.					
f_i	0	0	0	0	0	1	0	1	1
f_{i+1}	0	0	1	1	0	0	1	1	1
f_{i+2}	0	1	1	0	0	0	1	0	1
.				.					
.				.					
.				.					
f_j	0	0	1	0	0	0	1	1	1
f_{j+1}	0	1	1	1	0	0	1	1	1
.				.					
.				.					
.				.					

(a)

Cell Identification	Faults
.	.
.	.
.	.
001	f_i, f_{i+1}, f_j
.	.
.	.
.	.
101	f_{i+2}, f_{j+1}
.	.
.	.
.	.

(b)

Figure 5.5 (a) Simulation data. (b) Partial cell dictionary.

The reader has probably noticed the loss of diagnostic resolution associated with the above example. This is a general feature of cell dictionaries, since a fault can only be diagnosed to within one cell-full. Another drawback shows up when field diagnosis points to an unoccupied cell. Here we must either search neighboring cells to find a nearest occupied cell or we must resort to multiple cell dictionaries having different segment sizes.[6] The latter possibility is shown in Figure 5.6, where the vector of test results for f_i, lying at point A, falls in cell C_k which is unoccupied. We then go to a cell dictionary based on

[6] See the article by Chang and Thomis (1967).

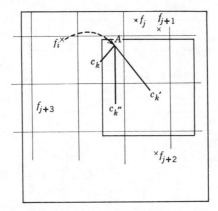

Figure 5.6   Use of multiple cell dictionaries.

bigger segments, and look again. This time, A is assigned to C'_k, which is also unoccupied. Finally, the search of even larger cells yields C''_k, which is occupied. This search has required considerable effort. Moreover, the diagnostic resolution is quite poor, since the fault is only identified as one of the set $\{f_i, f_j, f_{j+1}, f_{j+2}, f_{j+3}\}$.

5.4   Tradeoffs

In one sense, the final consumer of the services provided by automated diagnosis procedures is the field maintenance man. Consequently dictionaries should be evaluated from his viewpoint. Three of the major factors that will influence his opinion of a dictionary are its *accuracy, identification time*, and *diagnostic resolution*. We have already defined diagnostic resolution (in Subsection 2.1.3); accuracy refers to the fraction of system faults that can be diagnosed via the dictionary, and identification time refers to the average time required to proceed from a set of test results to a correct diagnosis. We comment briefly on these three factors before discussing tradeoffs between them.

Accuracy is not exclusively a function of the dictionary representation; it also depends on adequate design of the subject, proper design and encoding of the diagnostic procedures, and the use of adequate fault simulation methods. Accuracy would not be an issue if all of the assumptions mentioned in Section 5.1 were universally valid. We may therefore think of a dictionary as a device to improve the overall accuracy of the diagnostic process, in the face of defects in design, programming, and simulation which tend to degrade it.

Our second factor—the identification time—obviously depends on the bulk and format of the dictionary, and on the available accuracy and diagnostic

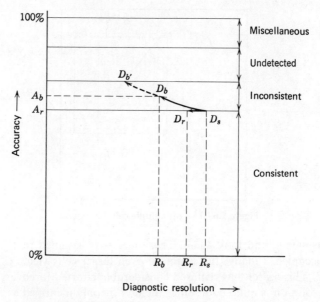

Figure 5.7   Curve of accuracy versus diagnostic resolution.

resolution. It strongly influences the average system repair time, and hence the total expected down-time over the life of the system.

The third and final factor—diagnostic resolution—has been considered elsewhere in this book. We point out here that adequate diagnostic resolution demands adequate numbers and placement of test points, effective diagnostic procedures, and the use of suitable dictionary representations. It is also closely related to the other two factors—accuracy and identification time. It is therefore helpful to examine the relationships between these three factors, since they may lead to tradeoffs which we can exploit (Chang, 1968b).

We first study the relationship between accuracy and diagnostic resolution, which is depicted in the hypothetical curve of Figure 5.7. The curve assumes that the set of subject faults has been split into four classes, according to the outcome of diagnosis:

1. The *inconsistent or mismatched* class, containing all faults that produce inconsistencies or mismatches.[7]

2. The *consistent* class, the complement of class 1.

3. The *undetected* class, containing all faults that are not detected by the diagnostic procedure at hand.

4. The *miscellaneous* class, containing the faults whose behavior could not be predicted by simulation, plus an assortment of other pathological cases.

---

[7] These terms are defined in Section 5.1.

A dictionary based on one of the straightforward representations can only diagnose faults of class 2. Hence the accuracy of such a dictionary is relatively low. This is shown by point D_s of Figure 5.7. The pseudo-random number representation is obtained by subjecting binary fault vectors to a pseudo-random data reduction procedure. As we noted in Subsection 5.2.2, this procedure may cause loss of diagnostic resolution. Hence the point D_r of Figure 5.7.

On the other hand, the back-up techniques of Section 5.3 attempt to increase accuracy by masking out the mismatched portions of fault vectors.[8] The overall effect is that accuracy is improved at the expense of diagnostic resolution, as point D_b of the Figure suggests. We must emphasize, however, that the possible improvement in accuracy is indeed limited: faults of the undetected and miscellaneous classes can never be diagnosed by clever manipulation of the test results. This point is illustrated by D_b', which shows the upper bound on accuracy. Further improvement would require a major overhaul of the subject's hardware design and diagnostic procedures; it is beyond the scope of *ad hoc* dictionary techniques.

Finally, Figure 5.7 suggests a possible tradeoff involving two types of dictionary. The primary dictionary would use exact-match techniques, yielding diagnosis of A_r faults with diagnostic resolution R_r. The secondary dictionary would use back-up techniques (phase or cell), and would diagnose an additional set $A_b - A_r$ of faults with lowered resolution R_b.

We now examine the relationship between diagnostic resolution and identification time. Here again, a hypothetical curve is helpful to show qualitative features. The first point, D_n of Figure 5.8, represents the case in which no dictionary whatsoever is used. Here the test results are interpreted manually. If the maintenance man happens to be a skilled technician who

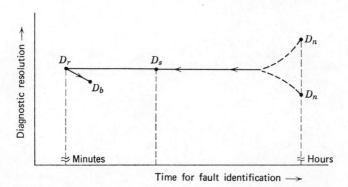

Figure 5.8 Curve of identification time versus diagnostic resolution.

---

[8] The relevance of this to inconsistent faults is easily established by noting that every inconsistent fault must, at some time, cause a dictionary mismatch.

knows the subject and the diagnostic procedures in great detail, the diagnostic resolution will be good. However, the identification time will be exceedingly long, as the coordinates of D_n indicate.

The use of even the simplest dictionary representations will drastically cut the identification time, as point D_s suggests. The pseudo-random representation further simplifies table look-up, hence point D_r. If the exact-match dictionary fails to yield a match, more time is needed to search a back-up dictionary. Moreover, manual processing of the test results (to create cell numbers) may be necessary. Hence the identification time increases to produce point D_b.

5.5 Summary

We have described several ways of processing simulation data to form fault dictionaries. Some of our techniques (the exact-match representations) were aimed solely at fast, error-free use of the simulation data by a relatively unskilled maintenance man. Others tried to help us with difficulties caused by the failure of some fundamental assumption. These techniques (the cell and phase representations) allowed us to diagnose some faults that cause inconsistencies and/or mismatches. However, none of these approaches is of the slightest help in treating undetected faults or faults that cause such wild behavior as to render the execution of a diagnosis procedure meaningless. A much more fundamental attack is required to cope with these problems. (Some results in this area were given in Section 4.4.) We now discuss some current research in unsolved problems—Chapter VI.

Recent Developments

In this chapter, we give an account of the current state of the fault diagnosis art. We do this by outlining a few of the many research studies that are being done in fault diagnosis. Our list of topics is not exhaustive, but it is representative of the current efforts in this area. However, most of the problems described are necessarily unsolved as of this date (late 1968).

We first discuss a favorite topic—current research in fault simulation (Section 6.1). Then we examine other areas in Section 6.2. Finally, we offer concluding comments and some speculations on the future (Section 6.3).

6.1 Recent Developments in Digital Fault Simulation

We pointed out some shortcomings of the Sequential Analyzer system in Subsection 4.4.3. Here we discuss recent developments aimed at rectifying these shortcomings. Some of these developments have been completed; others are still in progress. This material is taken from published and unpublished work by Armstrong (1969), Hardie and Suhocki (1967), Menon (1965), Manning and Chang (1967, 1968), and Schertz and Metze (1968).

6.1.1 Speed Improvement. First we discuss techniques aimed at speeding up digital fault simulation—probably the most pressing need of all.

(a) Macro "Gates." This technique was independently proposed by Hardie and Suhocki (1967), and by Seshu in unpublished work. The basic notion is to treat small, frequently used sequential circuits as gates. Thus a flip-flop (the obvious candidate for this treatment) is described to the simulation system as a "gate" of two inputs (SET and RESET) and two outputs. The logic compiler may treat such a gate by placing a link jump at the appropriate spot in the compiled simulator. This causes a transfer to a closed subroutine which updates a table of flip-flop states. This yields a saving in computation over the standard approach of simulating the flip-flop as a pair of cross-connected gates, under the condition that the particular flip-flop is fault free.

The technique has been implemented in both the Saturn Simulator of Hardie and Suhocki (using open subroutines), and the Sequential Analyzer. It has proved to be worthwhile in both systems. Currently the Analyzer allows only simple NOR and NAND flip-flops, whereas the Saturn Simulator permits the use of a variety of flip-floplike devices. Notice that the Analyzer's Huffman Analysis program is unaware of flip-flop feedback loops under this approach and thus bypasses the time-consuming task of performing race analysis. This is justified by noting that such loops usually change state much more rapidly than do the other varieties of feedback loops.

(*b*) *Fault Collapsing.* This technique, described by Schertz and Metze (1968), improves simulation speed by reducing the number of failed machines that must be simulated. The basic idea is to find sets of faults that cannot be distinguished by any possible test. We then replace all members of each set by a single, representative fault.

Certain sets of indistinguishable faults can be identified with types of gates. For example, an s–a–0 input to a NAND cannot possibly be distinguished from the output s–a–1 fault. Similarly, an s–a–0 NAND output will be detected by any one of the tests that check for s–a–1 (i.e. open) NAND inputs. Other sets result from the topology of the circuit, and require more extensive analysis. For example, if a gate A has fanout of 1 (say to a gate B), then an output-stuck failure of A cannot be distinguished from the corresponding input-stuck failure of B. In any event, one would like the logic compiler to identify all sets of indistinguishable faults, and to reduce the number of failed machines accordingly. Results obtained by studying several circuits indicate that this reduction could be drastic in many cases.

(*c*) *Selective Trace.* The selective trace idea was put forward by both Hardie and Suhocki (1967) and Menon (1965). One performs a simple test which asks whether a section of logic will change state during the events modelled by the current pass through the compiled simulator. If not, the part of the simulator devoted to that section of logic is bypassed.[1] Hardie and Suhocki have used this idea in connection with flip-floplike devices. A test comprising three instructions (are the SET and RESET inputs both inactive?) allows them to bypass a sequence of twelve instructions used to compute the new flip-flop state. Menon has implemented a more comprehensive version of the technique. He has observed experimentally that the simulation time for certain large decoders is cut by a factor of six through the use of selective trace—a worthwhile gain, indeed. We now turn to a more elaborate technique for speed improvement described by Manning and Chang (1968).

(*d*) *Functional Simulation.* Observe that the entire simulation process, as we have described it to this point, is conducted at the gate level of detail.

---

[1] Hardie and Suhocki call this technique "stimulus bypassing."

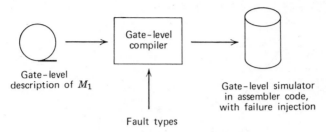

Figure 6.1   Simulation process I.

(We include macro gates as a minor extension of this assertion.) If we are attempting to deal with most or all of a large digital system, simulation time may be further cut by the following approach.

Suppose that the system is composed of several meaningful sections or modules, called $M_1, \ldots, M_n$. Also assume that we wish to determine overall system behavior in the presence of faults of M_1 only. Then it is clearly unnecessary to simulate $M_2, \ldots, M_n$ at the gate level of fine detail. A coarser approach called *functional simulation* will suffice. For example, a decoder need not be handled by computing the outputs of all constituent gates. We can simply compute the values of the Boolean expressions realized by the decoder. Similar remarks hold true for registers, sequential circuits, arithmetic units, channels, and so on. Note that functional simulation does not, in general, permit the insertion of faults, so that module M_1 must usually be treated at gate level. Nevertheless, intuition suggests that large gains may be made with this technique.

The basic approach we took was, first, to choose a small number of commonly-used functional modules. A concise, simple language for specifying the subject system in terms of these modules was designed. The user of the system would feed a source description written in this language to functional-level compilers, which would generate the simulation code. A linking loader would then combine the functional and gate-level simulators to produce a simulation routine for the entire subject. The overall process is illustrated in Figures 6.1 to 6.3. (A simpler approach would be to place the whole burden of

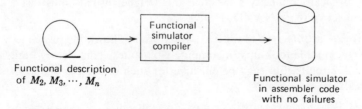

Figure 6.2   Simulation process II.

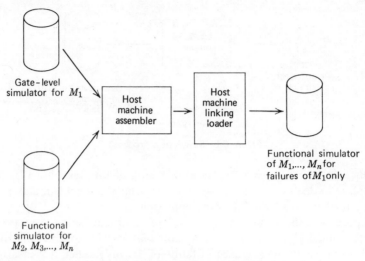

Figure 6.3 Simulation process III.

specifying types of functional modules and of generating simulation code on the shoulders of the user. This may do very well in a "one-shot" application. However, we felt that a general-purpose simulator could not tolerate the inconvenience to users and human error inherent in this approach.) We now discuss some details of our technique.

We chose the module types *decoder, sequential circuit* and *register-bus system*. We contend that most of a present-day digital system can be decomposed into modules of these types. The residue can always be simulated on the gate level. The simulation algorithms are as follows.

(i) FOR DECODERS. We minimize the given circuit with a Quine-McCluskey program and simulate the minimized circuit at gate level. (Alternately, we could do table-lookup if the tables were small enough.) The saving results from the smaller number of gates in the minimized circuit. This, in turn, is caused by failure of logic designers to minimize their designs, other design goals being more important. Also, we permit all Boolean connectives, whereas the designer usually must use a single connective (e.g., NAND, NOR).

(ii) FOR SEQUENTIAL CIRCUITS. We store the flowtable in memory, and perform table look-ups to compute next states. This clearly limits us to small circuits, but may be effective for such circuits as sequencers and small counters.

(iii) FOR REGISTER-BUS SYSTEMS. A collection of registers and their interconnecting busses is called a register-bus system. Thus the system inputs are data to be loaded in certain registers, plus gating signals. The outputs are the contents of various registers. We simulate such a system by allocating a memory area in the host machine corresponding to each register or bus. Whenever a gate signal is found to be active during simulation, the contents of one memory area are moved into another.

Since the simulator is not yet operational, we derived performance estimates as follows. For decoders, several specimens from existing computers were minimized by hand, and the simulation speeds before and after minimization were compared. Improvements of 30 to 60 percent were obtained. It is difficult to estimate the improvement obtainable with the sequential circuit technique. We can say nothing definite here.

Finally, the register-bus systems were evaluated as follows. First, the functional simulation routines were coded and timed, using the IBM 360/65 as host. For speed, these routines contain faster "short-cut" paths which are followed in certain special cases. Hence the relative frequencies of use of the various paths through the simulation routines had to be evaluated. To do this, a fault simulation on the gate level of a small asynchronous processor was studied. (This simulation involved more than 100 register transfers and 2500 processor faults.) The fault simulation output was analyzed to provide the necessary frequency-of-use statistics. The final result was an improvement in excess of 100 to 1 in simulation speed of register-bus systems.

Although this work is not yet completed, accounts of our progress have appeared in the references cited above. We feel that the results to date show that functional simulation can provide a good improvement in simulation speed. We have also established the feasibility of automatically compiling functional simulators from a suitable source language. An obvious extension of our techniques is to include arithmetic units, memories, and input-output channels.

(*e*) *Gate-level Simulation by Path Sensitizing.* The path-sensitizing methods of Section 3.1 were presented as techniques for deriving tests to detect a given fault of a combinational network. However, any one of them can be applied to the inverse problem, of computing the faults detected by a given test. (Indeed, we hinted broadly at this in the closing statements of Subsections 3.1.3 and 3.1.4, where the necessary algorithm was sketched.) Consequently, these methods provide ways of doing gate-level fault simulation, and are therefore potential competitors for the method given in Subsection 4.3.2. The choice will be made primarily on grounds of simulation speed. Certainly, there are circuits for which each approach has the edge. Hence more experimental data are needed to determine which method is favorable for the majority of commonly-simulated circuits. These data should soon be available, since programs employing path sensitizing for gate-level simulation are under construction by Armstrong (1969).

6.1.2 Other Improvements. The remaining shortcomings of the Analyzer are in modelling, capacity, and failure modes. Here, we summarize our view of future prospects in these areas.

Hardie and Suhocki (1967) have given a plausible method for modelling clocked *flip-flop realizations* (realizations having few or no global feedback loops, memory being achieved by flip-flops and flip-floplike devices). They first simulate the clock circuitry, followed by the combinational logic. The memory elements are treated last. Huffman analysis is obviously inappropriate here. The major type of misbehavior occurs when the SET and RESET inputs of a flip-flop are simultaneously active. This phenomenon is easy to monitor during simulation and the monitoring job is much simpler than Huffman analysis.

The above approach seems very good indeed if we can insist on the exclusive use of well-designed flip-flop realizations. However, many fault-simulation systems will be asked to deal with the much less tractable designs described in Subsection 4.4.3 (partially-clocked designs with abundant global feedback and overly long clock pulses, giving rise to a weird mixture of synchronous and asynchronous operation). The problem of modelling these adequately remains unsolved.

The problem of adequate capacity has diminished with the advent of virtual memory schemes backed by large quantities (5×10^5 words) of fast core memory and megaword amounts of bulk core. This trend toward huge, fast, cheap memories is expected to continue. This, and the use of functional simulation, will soon allow us easily to treat digital systems that have 10^5 or more gates.

Turning to failure modes, Chang has proposed a flexible tabular approach (Chang, 1969). This would allow the user of a simulation system to specify the permissible logical failure modes of his devices as small tables of input data. Common failure modes would be provided as system default options. However, failure modes giving rise to nonlogical phenomena have not yet been adequately dealt with. The classic example here is the time-varying intermittent fault. Finally, we cannot report any advances in heuristics for test generation. These last two points are therefore good topics for future work.

6.2 Recent Developments in Other Areas

Here we outline a very small sample of current research in fault diagnosis. Our choice of topics was dictated by personal interest and bias, and should not be interpreted to mean any more than that.

6.2.1 Hardware Compilers. Throughout this book, we have advocated the need for strict control over logic design in order to ensure "diagnosability" of the product. However, if we are to dictate to the logic designers, we must first have something to dictate. As we previously have pointed out, a set of design principles or constraints, which would guarantee diagnosability if followed rigorously, would be ideal here. Unfortunately, the principles put forth to date[2] are far from complete in this sense. Moreover, they are often restrictive (asynchronous, sequential-mode designs) or vague (well-modularized designs).

If we are to obtain better principles, we need a method to measure diagnosability (i.e., a fault simulator) plus a way to produce hardware designs subject to various design principles. At present, designs are produced by hand, which seems unsatisfactory. An automated design facility, or "Hardware Compiler," would produce designs more cheaply and quickly, and could be made to respect design constraints much more scrupulously than could a human designer. (We have always found logic designers to be notorious for their independence of views!)

Such a compiler, by analogy with software compilers, would accept a device-independent description of a system in some source language,[3] and would produce gate-level designs, subject to any desired constraints, as its output. It would thus allow many designs to be tried, and a search for a nearly-optimal design could be undertaken. A single (very skilled) system designer could do the whole design, hopefully leading to a more uniform and balanced result. A number of hardware compilers have been described; we shall describe an unfinished effort begun by Metze and Seshu (1966), and presently being carried on by Metze. Other notable projects have been done by Friedman T. D. (1967), by McCurdy and Chu (1967), by Gorman (1967), and by Srinivasan (1967).

The Computer Compiler (as the Seshu-Metze system is called) will consist of two parts: a hardware-independent system compiler (like a FORTRAN compiler) which produces strings of device-independent output, and a hardware compiler (like a FAP assembler) which produces a gate-level design. The system compiler has features such as MACRO, REPEAT, and library function calls, and produces a specification of machine structure in terms of time-ordered strings of microinstructions. This specification could be used as input to a simulator which would allow design verification and experimental programming. The hardware compiler does all Boolean minimization, which will become less important as Large-Scale Integrated circuitry becomes available.

[2] See Subsection 4.4.2.
[3] Versions of FORTRAN, ALGOL, PL/I and Iverson's language have all been proposed for this purpose. COBOL remains untried.

Subjects are described to the system compiler in two ways; the global description, and the descriptions of subsystems. The partitioning of the subject into subsystems must be done by the system designer, keeping the desirability of well-modularized designs firmly in mind. The global description specifies subsystems which may operate concurrently, plus global parameters such as word lengths. Each subsystem description contains declarations of registers, which are analogous to PL/I DECLARE statements or FORTRAN DIMENSION statements. The registers that lie on the INTERFACE between subsystems must be identified as such, since the transmission of information between subsystems that can run concurrently must be carefully controlled by the compiler. The rest of a subsystem description is analogous to the "program flow" of a FORTRAN program, and contains register transfer (assignment) statements, decode (computed GO TO) statements, and subsystem calls (subroutine calls) whereby one subsystem can activate another. However, the analogy is imperfect here, since a flag flip-flop is always used to interlock the operation of the calling and called subsystems. This interlock resembles the PL/I ON facility. Finally, note that all passing of parameters (operands and instructions) is via interface registers.

The output of the system compiler is strings of microinstructions, one string per subsystem. These strings include the usual Boolean operators, microinstructions to start or finish a register transfer, and branches to other microinstructions. A certain amount of processing is done to introduce as much concurrency into the strings as is possible.

In summary, the authors of the Computer Compiler feel that it should be able to optimize designs extensively, while maintaining the modularity specified in the input text, as well as strictly observing design constraints. It should therefore prove to be a useful tool in the development of principles for diagnosable design.

6.2.2   Fault Diagnosis without Simulation.   In Chapter II, we stated that a major milestone in fault diagnosis occurred when workers began to test the subject's *hardware* rather than its *functions*. However, we mentioned in a footnote that there is no philosophical objection to the testing of machine functions. Instead, the problem lay in the practical impossibility of completely testing the complex functions (e.g., arithmetic operations) which were considered. Clearly, if simple machine functions which could be exhaustively tested could be found, this objection would evaporate. Moreover, fault simulation might be unnecessary, since the subject's behavior under failure could be predicted directly from knowledge of the functions and interconnections involved. At any rate, any simulation would be on a functional rather than gate level.

One step in this direction was made by Manning (1966b), who observed that a detection sequence for a certain asynchronous control unit could be written down by inspection, without knowledge of the hardware involved. This was because the control unit was an interconnection of functionally simple units called control points.[4] A detection sequence for a control point was simple and obvious, and control points were in one-to-one correspondence with the microinstructions processed by the control unit. Hence the observation.

Marlett (1966) extended this reasoning further, and was able to characterize control point failures in terms of the resulting control point behaviors. This, in turn, allowed him to predict the action of the entire control unit in the presence of such a failure. Again, this allowed him to say that certain register transfers or arithmetic operations would or would not occur, in the presence of such a failure. Therefore, the special structure of the control allowed him to construct a diagnostic procedure for it, without doing fault simulation. For the future, one must find ways to extend this approach to cover failures outside of the control unit. It would also be helpful to find a wider class of realizations which lend themselves to this approach. Nevertheless, this seems to us to be a novel and promising approach to the problem of fault diagnosis.

6.2.3   Structural Studies in Fault Diagnosis.   In a remarkable and interesting paper, C. V. Ramamoorthy (1967) considers the application of graph theory to diagnosis problems. He begins by associating the nodes of a directed graph with the components (gates, modules, subsystems, etc.) of a digital system. Edges of the graph correspond to signal paths. Next, a previous result is applied to permit partitioning of the system into combinational and sequential subsystems (link and maximal strongly connected subgraphs, respectively). We have seen in Section 3.4 that this process is often done to facilitate the writing of tests; Ramamoorthy's result allows us to do it automatically rather than manually. The algorithm (which operates on the connectivity matrix of the graph) requires no matrix multiplication or partitioning; thus we might be able to partition quite large systems automatically.

Next, the problem of test point placement is considered. The use of the Quine-McCluskey algorithm to select a minimal set of test points is demonstrated. By defining the *range* of an input-output pair of test points to be the set of nodes lying on directed paths between the input and output points, something can be said about indistinguishability (cf. Subsection 6.1.1). Namely, nodes are indistinguishable if they belong to the same set of ranges and no others. This result, of course, deliberately ignores the behavioral side of the picture: test outcomes.

---

[4] See, for instance, the Appendix of Manning (1966a) for a description of the control and the control points.

Another problem is that of identifying or opening feedback loops. We saw in Section 4.2 that this must be done to allow partial ordering of the gates of a circuit before compiling a simulator. We prefer that a minimal set of loops be opened (to reduce the processing done in Huffman Analysis), and that all gates remain reachable from the primary inputs (to permit testing of all gates). Under these constraints, Ramamoorthy gives a simple, fast algorithm for determining a minimal set of loops. The only shortcoming is that the algorithm becomes semiexhaustive if an additional condition placed on the graph is violated.

Finally, comments on self-diagnosis of a processor and on the "best" order to test system components are given. The paper is impressive for two reasons: first, the final results are interesting and of practical use. Also, a great deal of our present knowledge in fault diagnosis is qualitative and vague. It is therefore encouraging to see progress in applying mathematical techniques to these problems.

6.3   Speculations on the Future

It is always risky to prophesy, but this seems to inhibit very few authors—ourselves included! We feel that the sheer growth in numbers of computers will force much greater automation of fault diagnosis procedures than we have seen to date. In addition, the shift from batched mode to real-time and time-shared modes of operation will cause more interest in automated fault diagnosis. For these applications, we shall see increasingly clever blends of diagnosis and redundancy technologies, to permit survival in the face of failures. The pioneering work of Avizienis et al. (1968) will probably point the way to many of these developments. Finally, we expect to see a program of research in the application of graph theory, algebra, and combinatorial analysis to diagnosis problems, following the initial steps taken by Ramamoorthy. We feel that the outstanding problems in fault diagnosis can be properly understood and solved only when this is done.

References

Amar, V., and N. Condulmari (1967), "Diagnosis of Large Combinational Networks," *IEEE Trans. on Electronic Computers*, **EC-16**, 675–680.

Armstrong, D. B. (1966), "On Finding a Nearly Minimal Set of Fault Detection Tests for Combinational Logic Nets," *IEEE Trans. on Electronic Computers*, **EC-15**, 66–73.

Armstrong, D. B. (1969), unpublished work.

Avizienis, A., D. A. Rennels, and J. A. Rohr (1968), "Application of Concurrent Diagnosis and Replacement in a Self-Repairing Computer," *Digest of 1968 IEEE International Convention*, p. 195.

Bashkow, T. R., J. Friets, and A. Karson (1963), "A Programming System for Detection and Diagnosis of Machine Malfunctions," *IEEE Trans. on Electronic Computers*, **EC-12**, 10–17.

Booth, T. L. (1967), *Sequential Machines and Automata Theory*, Wiley, New York.

Breuer, M. A. (1968), "Fault Detection in a Linear Cascade of Identical Sequential Machines," *Proc. 9th Ann. Switching Automata Theory Symp.*

Brule, J. D., R. A. Johnson, and E. J. Kletsky (1960), "Diagnosis of Equipment Failures," *IRE Trans. on Reliability and Quality Control*, **RQC-9**, 23–34.

Brown, R. M. (1964), "The CSX-1 Computer," *IEEE Trans. on Electronic Computers*, **EC-13**, 247–250.

Caldwell, S. H. (1958), *Switching Circuits and Logical Design*, Wiley, New York.

Carter, W. C., H. C. Montgomery, R. J. Preiss, and H. J. Reinheimer (1964), "Design of Serviceability Features for the IBM System/360," *IBM Journal of Research and Development*, **8**(2), 115–126.

Chang, H. Y. (1965), "An Algorithm for Selecting an Optimum Set of Diagnostic Tests," *IEEE Trans. on Electronic Computers*, **EC-14**(5), 706–711.

Chang, H. Y. (1968a), "A Distinguishability Criterion for Selecting Efficient Diagnostic Tests," *AFIPS Proc. of Spring Joint Computer Conference*, **32**, 529–534.

Chang, H. Y. (1968b), "Figures of Merit for the Diagnostics of a Digital System," *IEEE Trans. on Reliability*, **R-17**(3), 147–153.

Chang, H. Y. (1969), "A Method for Digitally Simulating Shorted Input Diode Failures," *Bell System Technical Journal*, **48**(6), 1957–1966.

Chang, H. Y., and W. Thomis (1967), "Methods of Interpreting Diagnostic Data for Locating Faults in Digital Machines," *Bell System Technical Journal*, **46**(2), 289–317.

Cohen, J. J., and L. A. Whitaker (1960), "Improved Techniques in Diagnostic Programming," *The Sylvania Technologist*, **13**(3), 90–96.

Daggett, N. L., and E. S. Rich (1953), "Diagnostic Programs and Marginal Checking in Whirlwind I Computer," *IRE National Convention Record*, Pt. 7, pp. 48–54.

Dent, J. J. (1968), "Diagnostic Engineering Requirements," *AFIPS Proc. of Spring Joint Computer Conference*, **32**, 503–508.

Downing, R. W., J. S. Nowak, and L. S. Tuomenoksa (1964), "No. 1 ESS Maintenance Plan," *Bell System Technical Journal*, **43**, 1961–2019.

Eckert, J. P., Jr. (1953), "Checking Circuits and Diagnostic Routines," *IRE National Convention Record*, Pt. 7, pp. 62–65.

Eldred, R. D. (1959), "Test Routines Based on Symbolic Logic Statements," *Journal of ACM*, **6**(1), 33–36.

Estrin, G. (1953), "Diagnosis and Prediction of Malfunctions in the Computing Machine at the Institute for Advanced Study," *IRE International Convention Record*, Pt. 7, pp. 59–61.

Forbes, R. E., D. H. Rutherford, C. B. Stieglitz, and L. H. Tung (1965), "A Self-Diagnosable Computer," *AFIPS Proc. of the Fall Joint Computer Conference*, **27** (Part 1), 1073–1086.

Friedman, A. D. (1967), "Fault Detection in Redundant Circuits," *IEEE Trans. on Electronic Computers*, **EC-16**(1), 99–100.

Friedman, T. D. (1967), "ALERT: A Program to Compile Logic Designs of New Computers," *Digest of First Annual IEEE Computer Conference*, pp. 128–130.

Galey, J. M., R. E. Norby, and J. P. Roth (1964), "Techniques for the Diagnosis of Switching Circuit Failures," *IEEE Trans. on Communication and Electronics*, **33**(74), 509–514.

Gill, A. (1962), *Introduction to the Theory of Finite-State Machines*, McGraw-Hill, New York.

Gorman, D. F. (1967), "Systems Level Design Automation: A Progress Report on the System Descriptive Language (SDL II)," *Digest of First Annual IEEE Computer Conference*, pp. 131–134.

Hackl, F. J., and R. W. Shirk (1965), "An Integrated Approach to Automated Computer Maintenance," 1965 *IEEE Conference Record on Switching Circuit Theory and Logical Design*, pp. 289–300.

Hardie, F. H., and R. J. Suhocki (1967), "Design and Use of Fault Simulation for Saturn Computer Design," *IEEE Trans. on Electronic Computers*, **EC-16**(4), 412–429.

Hennie, F. C. (1964), "Fault Detection Experiments for Sequential Circuits," *Proc. 5th Annual Symp. on Switching Theory and Logical Design*, pp. 95–110.

Hennie, F. C. (1968), *Finite-State Models for Logical Machines*, Wiley, New York.

Huffman, D. A. (1954), "The Synthesis of Sequential Switching Circuits," *Journal of the Franklin Institute*, **257**(3, 4), 161–190, 275–303.

Iverson, K. E. (1966), *A Programming Language*, Wiley, New York.

Johnson, R. A., E. Kletsky, and J. Brule (1959), "Diagnosis of Equipment Failures," Syracuse University Research Institute Technical Report I. (AD-213876).

Johnson, R. A. (1960), "An Information Theory Approach to Diagnosis," *Proc. 6th National Symp. on Reliability and Quality Control*, pp. 102–109.

Jones, E. R., and C. H. Mays (1967), "Automatic Test Generation Methods for Large Scale Integrated Logic," *IEEE Journal of Solid State Circuits*, **SC-2**, 221–226.

Kautz, W. H. (1967), "Fault Diagnosis in Combinational Digital Circuits," *Digest of First Annual IEEE Computer Conference*, pp. 2–5.

Kautz, W. H. (1968), "Fault Testing and Diagnosis in Combinational Digital Circuits," *IEEE Transactions on Computers*, **EC-17**(4), 352–366.

Kime, C. R. (1966), "An Organization for Checking Experiments on Sequential Circuits," *IEEE Transactions on Electronic Computers*, **EC-15**, 113–115.

Kletsky, E. J. (1960), "An Application of the Information Theory Approach to

Failure Diagnosis," *IRE Trans. on Reliability and Quality Control*, **RQC-9**, 29–39.

Kohavi, Z., and P. Lavallée (1967a), "Design of Diagnosable Sequential Machines," *AFIPS Proc. of Spring Joint Computer Conference*, **30**, 713–718.

Kohavi, Z., and P. Lavallée (1967b), "Design of Sequential Machines with Fault Detection Capabilities," *IEEE Trans. on Electronic Computers*, **EC-16**(4), 473–484.

Kruskal, J. B., and R. E. Hart (1966), "A Geometric Interpretation of Diagnostic Data from a Digital Machine, Based on a Study of the Morris, Illinois Electronic Central Office," *Bell System Technical Journal*, **45**, 1299–1338.

Maling, K., and E. L. Allen, Jr. (1963), "A Computer Organization and Programming System for Automated Maintenance," *IEEE Trans. on Electronic Computers*, **EC-12**, 887–895.

Mandelbaum, D. (1964), "A Measure of Efficiency of Diagnostic Tests upon Sequential Logic," *IEEE Trans. on Electronic Computers*, **EC-13**, 630.

Manning, E. G. (1966a), "On Computer Self-Diagnosis; Part I—Experimental Study of a Processor," *IEEE Trans. on Electronic Computers*, **EC-15**(6), 873–881.

Manning, E. G. (1966b), "On Computer Self-Diagnosis; Part II—Generalizations and Design Principles," *IEEE Trans. on Electronic Computers*, **EC-15**(6), 882–890.

Manning, E. G., and H. Y. Chang (1967), "A Comparison of Fault Simulation Methods for Digital Systems," *Digest of the First Annual IEEE Computer Conference*, pp. 10–13.

Manning, E. G., and H. Y. Chang (1968), "Functional Techniques for Efficient Digital Fault Simulation," *1968 IEEE International Convention Digest*, p. 194.

Marlett, R. A. (1966), "On the Design and Testing of Self-Diagnosable Computers," Report R-293, Coordinated Science Laboratory, University of Illinois, Urbana, Illinois.

McCluskey, E. J., Jr. (1956), "Minimization of Boolean Functions," *Bell System Technical Journal*, **35**, 1417–1444.

McCluskey, E. J., Jr. (1965), *Introduction to the Theory of Switching Circuits*, McGraw-Hill, New York.

McCurdy, B. D., and Y. Chu (1967), "Boolean Translation of a Macro Logic Design," *Digest of First Annual IEEE Computer Conference*, pp. 124–127.

Meagher, R. E., and J. P. Nash (1952), "The ORDVAC," *Review of Electronic Digital Computers*, pp. 37–43.

Mealy, G. E. (1955), "A Method of Synthesizing Sequential Circuits," *Bell System Technical Journal*, **34**, 1045–1079.

Menon, P. R. (1965), "A Simulation Program for Logic Networks," *Bell Telephone Laboratories Internal Technical Memorandum*, No. MM 65-1271-3.

Metze, G., and S. Seshu (1966), "A Proposal for a Computer Compiler," *AFIPS Proc. of the Spring Joint Computer Conference*, **28**, 253–263.

Miller, R. E. (1966), *Switching Theory*, Vols. I and II, Wiley, New York.

Moore, E. F. (1956), "Gedanken Experiments on Sequential Machines," *Automata Studies*, Princeton University Press, pp. 129–153.

Muller, D. E., and W. S. Bartky (1959), "A Theory of Asynchronous Circuits," *Proc. of International Symp. on the Theory of Switching*, Vol. 29 of the Annals of the Computation Laboratory of Harvard University, pp. 204–243, Harvard University Press.

Muller, D. E. (1967), "Evaluation of Logical and Organizational Methods for Improving the Reliability and Availability of a Computer," *Digest of First Annual IEEE Computer Conference*, pp. 53–55.

Poage, J. F. (1963), "Derivation of Optimal Tests to Detect Faults in Combinational Circuits," *Mathematical Theory of Automata*, Polytechnic Press, Brooklyn, N.Y., pp. 483–528.

Poage, J. F., and E. J. McCluskey (1964), "Derivation of Optimum Test Sequences for Sequential Machines," *5th Annual Symp. on Switching Theory and Logical Design*, pp. 121–132.

Preparata, F. P., G. Metze, and R. T. Chien (1967), "On the Connection Assignment Problem of Diagnosable Systems," *IEEE Transactions on Electronic Computers*, **EC-16**, 848–854.

Ramamoorthy, C. V. (1967), "A Structural Theory of Machine Diagnosis," *Proc. of Spring Joint Computer Conference*, **30**, 743–756.

Roth, J. P. (1966), "Diagnosis of Automata Failures: A Calculus and A Method," *IBM Journal of Research and Development*, **10**, 278–291.

Roth, J. P., W. G. Bouricius, and P. R. Schneider (1967), "Programmed Algorithms to Compute Tests to Detect and Distinguish Between Failures in Logic Circuits," *IEEE Trans. on Electronic Computers*, **EC-16**, 5, pp. 567–579.

Roth, J. P., and E. G. Wagner (1959), "Algebraic Topological Methods for the Synthesis of Switching Systems. Part III—Minimization of Nonsingular Boolean Trees," *IBM Journal of Research and Development*, **3**, 326–44.

Schertz, D. R., and G. Metze (1968), "On the Indistinguishability of Faults in Digital Systems," *Proc. 6th Annual Allerton Conf. on Circuit and System Theory*, 752–760.

Schneider, P. R. (1967), "On the Necessity to Examine *D*-Chains in Diagnostic Test Generation—An Example," *IBM Journal of Research and Development*, **11**(1), 114.

Seshu, S. (1964), "The Logic Organizer and Diagnosis Programs," Report R-226, Coordinated Science Laboratory, University of Illinois, Urbana, Ill. (AD-05927).

Seshu, S. (1965), "On An Improved Diagnosis Program," *IEEE Trans. on Electronic Computers*, **EC-14**(1), 76–79.

Seshu, S., and D. N. Freeman (1962), "The Diagnosis of Asynchronous Sequential Switching Systems," *IRE Trans. on Electronic Computers*, **EC-11**(4), 459–465.

Seshu, S., and R. Waxman (1966), "Fault Isolation in Conventional Linear Systems—A Feasibility Study," *IEEE Trans. on Reliability*, **R-15**(1), 11–16.

Shannon, C. E. (1948), "A Mathematical Theory of Communication," *Bell System Technical Journal*, **27**, 379–423, 623–656.

Srinivasan, C. V. (1967), "An Introduction to CDL1, A Computer Description Language," RCA Laboratories, Scientific Report No. 1, AFCRL-67-0565.

Suda, R. (1967), "An Application-Oriented Multiprocessing System: V. The Diagnostic Monitor," *IBM System Journal*, **6**(2), 116–123.

Torng, H. C. (1965), *Introduction to the Logical Design of Switching Systems*, Addison-Wesley, Reading, Mass.

Tsiang, S. H., and W. Ulrich (1962), "Automatic Trouble Diagnosis of Complex Logic Circuits," *Bell System Technical Journal*, **41**, 1177–1200.

Unger, S. H. (1959), "Hazards and Delays in Asynchronous Sequential Switching Circuits," *IRE Trans. on Circuit Theory*, **CT-6**, 12–25.

Walters, L. R. (1953), "Diagnostic Programming Techniques for the IBM Type 701 E.D.P.M.," *IRE National Convention Record*, Pt. 7, pp. 55–59.

Wheeler, D. J., and J. E. Robertson (1953), "Diagnostic Programs for the Illiac," *Proceedings of IRE*, **41,** 1320–1325.

Wilkes, M. V., M. Phister, and S. A. Barton (1953), "Experience with Marginal Checking and Automatic Routing of the EDSAC," *IRE National Convention Record*, Pt. 7, pp. 66–71.

Index